# Acclaim for Bob Palm

"I found it! When I was a kid, I lived in this Zone that Bob Palmer perfectly describes in his book. Somewhere along the path, I lost it. As a gifted athlete, I found it tremendously frustrating, not ever being able to reach the potential that matched my full ability. I tried practicing harder...generally a waste of time and effort. I tried positive attitude...didn't work. I tried taking lessons from the Masters...got worse. I tried sports psychology...got MUCH worse. Now after practicing Bob's methods, I have it again and know how to keep it, or as he says, 'to stay in the Zone'. As a retired US Navy SEAL and athlete, who has been able to get to the highest levels that my physical ability could take me in many sports, I will tell you that what Bob has learned and is teaching in this book is what you have been seeking. Read it, learn it, practice it, become the Zone! IT'S A LOT OF FUN!!"

> — **DR. JOE LACAZE**, Retired US Navy Seal, Doctor of Chiropractic, Certified Neuromuscular Therapist, NASM Performance Enhancement Specialist, Flexibility Specialist, and College Biomechanics Instructor

"Masterfully written!! It should be on the must read list of every serious competitor in any sport."

> — **STEVE BROWN**, Certified NSCA Level III Instructor, Chief Instructor at Ark-La-Tex School of Wing Shooting

"Since working with Bob late last year, not only have we made an improvement to my mental game, but I also have a much better understanding of the feel of the Zone."

— **PAUL GIAMBRONE III**, Master Level NSSA Instructor, 13 time world-champion and Owner of Giambrone Shooting Clinics

"Bob was the first mental coach that I worked with at the beginning of my career. His methods became some of the fundamentals that I used as part of my everyday routine. The knowledge that I have learned from him has helped me achieve my ultimate dream."

— **VINCENT HANCOCK,** Two-time Olympic Gold Medalist, Beijing and London – International Skeet

"Thanks Bob. I haven't felt this focused in years, maybe forever. When I was shooting I heard nothing. It was almost like the "Love of the Game" with Kevin Costner."

— **BRAD COLLINS**, American Skeet

"When we look at how nicely Bob Palmer's peak performance strategies meshed with our OSP System, where nothing was opposed in terms of our teaching style, our relationships with our students, our commitment for lifelong learning and our commitment to building the whole person, our own system has never been stronger and the future never brighter."

— **GIL AND VICKI ASH,** OSP Shooting School

"After only one season working with Bob Palmer, I had very consistent control of my nerves in every match. I was on-fire in August and podiumed alongside two of the best skeet shooters in the world. My overall improvement has been huge and in the World Skeet Championships I placed in the top 30 shooters in the world. This is an 80% improvement over the previous year."

— **ANDY SPOONER**, American Skeet

"Bob Palmer has worked with the elite shooters of my Youth Development Shotgun Team. Not only was there a remarkable transformation of the individual shooters, but also a strong team bonding. He will continue to be an integral part of our training program."

— **LES GREEVY**, USA shooting, Olympic Shooting Coach of the Year 2004

"I had a great State shoot - best one ever. Bob, you have really done a great job for me. I was always told that shooting was 99% mental and 1% ability. I guess at sixty it was the right time for me to invest in my mental game."

— **PAT LAIB**, ATA Trap

"I just wanted to let you know and say thanks for teaching me how to get in the Zone. The more people you teach the harder it will be to have the advantage over those who don't know. Thanks again."

— **JOHN CAFFEY,** ATA Trap

"The SportExcel strategies have become a part of me and a part of my clients. As a shooting coach, my teaching now goes way beyond mechanics where I'm now helping my clients get into the Zone in all aspects of their lives."

— **JIM SARKAUSKAS**, NSCA Certified Level II Instructor, Owner - The Rancho del Zorro Shooting Academy

"Thanks to Bob Palmer's high performance program, I'm at a place that is fantastically beautiful when it comes to shooting. I had a great year. I started at an average level and stepped it up every month. I had the best Grand (ATA Trap) I ever had. I even made the November 2011 cover of Trap & Field Magazine, a long time goal!"

— **MIKE WESTJOHN**, ATA Trap

"Before your program, I passively watched my son participate in sports and gave no thought to the impact that I was having. After taking your course, I will no longer just watch. I will continue to contribute positively to his mental game. My wife and I now have an active role that we never had before and it makes a considerable difference. Thanks for the work you have put into this program and we would recommend it to anyone wanting to advance, regardless of the endeavor."

— **GREG ELLIOTT**, Parent of a young Skeet shooter, U.S.

# Mind vs Target

## Six steps to winning in the clay target mind field

## Bob Palmer

SportExcel Inc

ISBN: 978-0-9917618-1-4

# Disclaimer

The information contained in this book is made available by SportExcel Inc. It is to be used strictly for educational purposes only. SportExcel Inc. does not offer any psychological, professional, medical, financial, personal or legal advice and none of the information contained in this book should be confused as such advice. Results of using the System may vary from individual to individual.

*For Caron and her inspiration and dedication to this project*

# Acknowledgments

Grateful acknowledgment is made to the following people for their contribution in the writing and creation of this book:

**Robert VandenDool** for creating the original artwork for the book cover and for providing creative collaboration on the cover design

**Andy Rouse** Wildlife Photography, UK for the rights to use his photograph of a lion's eye as a basis for the original cover artwork

**Caron Palmer** for project management and cover design

**Marg. Bruineman** for her sage editing

**Steve Brown** for setting me straight on many technical items

**Peter Gzowski** for the original inspiration to become a writer

**Vicki St. George** for her professional collaboration on the book

**Dr. John Grinder and Derek Balmer** for their inspirational NLP concepts

**Terry Heeg** Editor of Trap and Field Magazine for giving me the opportunity to write

**Sensei Masaru Shintani and my other senseis** for inspiring me to dig deep and figure it out

# Contents

## The SportExcel System

## Step 1 – Finding Your Zone   *10*

## Step 2 – Outcomes Alive!   *30*

## Step 3 – Guidance is like GPS   *55*

# Contents

# Foreword

If there was something you could do to give yourself the advantage in your performance that is undetectable in saliva, blood or urine by any lab or testing device of modern sports authorities, would you do it? We're talking about something that is going to make you stand out from the rest and improve your performance almost overnight so that it shows in your results and gets people talking and suspicious. We are speaking about something that will not only have people noticing your results but noticing how different you are from the last competition, and may even start asking questions such as what vitamins are you taking — or worse. And we are talking about something that is undetectable, period.

And did I say you'd look different, taller; your muscles will appear to be more defined; you will walk taller and speak with authority and confidence. Come on. Would you do this if no saliva, blood, urine or genetic test could detect the minutest trace of this, and it would give you a significant advantage over your opponents, give you incredible visual acuity, strength and absolute focus, totally undetectable by anyone in anyway? Would you be tempted?"

Well, fortunately, I'm not talking about ethics or drugs or cheating here. But I am talking about the Zone and the revolutionary way it gives you excellence in your game. So don't just read—learn — and allow Bob to teach you this very basic concept of the Zone.

— **DON KWASNYCIA,** Skeet Coach and Past Canadian Olympian

# Why You Need This Book

*Don't Think, Just Shoot:*

*A system test driven by champions*

*"When I step onto the court, I don't have to think about anything."*

— *Michael Jordan, Star Basketball Player*

As a high performance strategist and trainer who has worked with Olympic medalists in two sports, champions in many other sports and has 20 years of experience, I thought I'd introduce myself to the clay target shooters who read this book so you have an idea who Bob Palmer is and what I (he) has to offer as compared to most "off the shelf" books or programs on mental performance.

I am a martial artist, a fourth degree black belt and have only been clay target shooting three or four times. Shocked? Well, I participate in very few of the sports in which I work with athletes. For example, I don't snowboard but one of my snowboarders won silver in Vancouver 2010. And I don't surf, but one of my surfers recently podiumed in a world-class championship.

I've worked with shotgunners for over a decade, from North America — Canada, USA, and Mexico — to Great Britain and now Australia. What do they see in my program? Great results, podium finishes, cash prizes and a reconnection with the fun of the game.

How is my approach, and this book, different? Well, here is a scenario of the typical skeet shooter before he reads this book. His round is about to begin so he follows the advice of a mental-game book he purchased. (Pick any book, as they are all saying pretty much the same thing.) It told him to be positive so he smiles and struts his stuff. It said to use positive self-talk so he repeats over and over, "I am a great shot and I'll do well and I'll smoke targets." He tells himself, "It's one shot at a time, one shot at a time."

…He thinks about shooting 100s and winning HOA but he read that that was wrong, and he remembers, "one shot at time" and "process rather than outcome." He remembers to be positive and struts again, and then he says, "I'm great, just shoot." He remembers to calm himself with a deep breath that is a part of his pre-shot routine. He calls for the target and smokes the first station and goes through the same process for station two. He straightens his posture and tells himself, "One shot at a time," but the HOA thought creeps in and he shuts it down by remembering to breathe.

…Over and over, station two through seven, same pattern and he smokes them all. This is working! On station eight the thought of the perfect round creeps in and he remembers to say, "One shot at a time." And to strut. And to be positive. And to say, "I can do it." He smokes station eight, chipping just one. Phew. This is working. Five minutes before round two. Strut some more, breathe, "I'm good, I'm good. I can do it." These last paragraphs might have exhausted you. Just writing them did me in. This kind of mental approach, although typical, is way too much thinking and way too much to remember. But that is the kind of advice you typically get for your mental game. I find it difficult to imagine shooting four rounds or 10 stations this way or, for that matter, two, three or four days in a row and the potential shoot-offs that will be required, depending on the sport. This "thinking" approach is unsustainable. Shooting each shot like it is the only one, using positive self-talk and trying to think positive are the fastest ways down the tubes in any sport. I know. I've worked in more than 20 different sports, 30 if you count all the clay target disciplines. There has to be another way, a better way. And there is.

All this confusion around the mental game was created by observations of professional athletes who often learned to be high performers with very little idea of how they did it. So they either make it sound easy — just do it — or difficult — it is a lot of hard work — without actually giving any strategies on how to get there. It is actually quite easy to improve your shooting game if you follow one basic rule.

It is: **Don't think**. Following all the "thinking" advice of various books will exhaust you. It might work for a round or two, but you will start thinking so much that it will affect the technical side of your sport — stances, hold points, quiet eye, gun mounts, etc.

I've been teaching my systems approach for more than 20 years and recently put it to the test with one of the best shooters in skeet, a phenom by the name of Paul Giambrone III. Now Paul doesn't need any help from me. Believe me. But a client of mine told me about Paul and I looked up his website. It was a funny story because I was looking for an older man, perhaps balding, and that is exactly what I saw. A website photo showed an older gentleman teaching a young man in his twenties, and when I finally met Paul in an internet video call over Skype, I was shocked as the 'older man' I'd seen turned out to be Paul's student and Paul was the young man.

My first conversation with Paul amazed me. At 26 years of age he was already displaying the wisdom of coaches twice his age. I asked if this skeet shooter and coach would put my system to the test. He agreed and we went through the six steps of the program and the many strategies. Upon finishing, he told me that he was already using the types of tools I had taught him, but my system allowed him to use them sooner, to refine his game and to have no doubt as to whether he was in his Zone (high performance mode), or not.

Elite athletes and how they think (or don't think) are the model for my high performance system — football, hockey, baseball, snowboarding — and athletes like Paul are an important test. So I'd like to rewrite that earlier paragraph. Remember my earlier exhausting paragraph with all that thinking that came out of reading a book on the mental game? Well, here it is from the point of view of Paul as he competes in the shoot-off on station four:

**Paul:**  Pull. [Nothing else to report here.]

I have to apologize for such a short paragraph from Paul as he is intelligent and he does have a lot to say when he is off the station. Rather, his routines are so ingrained that he does no conscious thinking when on the station and in the shooting process. None. And to him, sometimes it even seems like he is along for the enjoyable ride and that his body is just a shooting machine. No deep breathing, no self-talk and no being positive. He just IS and he DOES consistently smoke targets.

[Note: Steve Brown, a wing-shooting coach from East Texas, says that in sporting clays, for example, there is some "talk" where the shooter might use a word or two to 'pace' himself, because, he notes, "unlike skeet, some presentations in sporting clays are of a much longer duration. From the time the shooter calls pull, until the second shot, the pair can sometimes stretch out over 8 seconds".  I consider that self-coaching, not thinking or self-talk.]

If you find a non-thinking approach in anyway interesting, I suppose that you'd like to learn to be a shooting machine like Paul. Well, read on, as you are about to find out some of the strategies that make my system so powerful and easy to use. I'll get you started and teach you how to NOT think, right from the get-go in STEP 1 of the SportExcel System. In the interim, take your last, conscious deep breath, as I expect your game — and your understanding of it — will never be the same.

— **Bob Palmer,**

**Barrie, Ontario**

# 1 Learning to Win

*The heights this book will take you, if you are willing to*

*stop thinking and just shoot*

*"We are what we repeatedly do. Excellence then, is not an act, but a habit."*

**— Aristotle, Star Philosopher**

Let's not mince words. The main goal of this book is to help you to win in your shooting game, whether that means winning competition HOAs, winning at the club level so that you can hold your head high or winning at the improvement game through on-going class punches. And although winning is the ultimate goal, enjoyment of your shooting sport is what is going to drive you to that perfect victory. The combined forces of winning and enjoyment are inseparable. It affects everything about your game, from the folks who you want to shoot with to the financial impact of earning a few payouts, from the type of shotguns you buy to your commitment to practice, attend competitions and put in your time.

Whether you are a novice or a professional, this book will help you create your own definition of high performance in order to win. From the get-go, I'll make no promises that this book will help you to win a world championship or even the club championship but you will have the tools and a system to do so. And I challenge you to see if you can apply them as effectively as the many champions I have worked with have done. Only you can dictate that along with how you read and apply this book to help you succeed in your goal.

# The Starting Point

This book is the starting point where you will understand what you learned or didn't learn from all your competitive experience, from playing Little League baseball, football, hockey or other sports, to your latest attempts to win in clay target sports. High performance is the process of doing anything well. In shooting, it is staying sharp, target after target, and understanding the nature of the distractions that conspire to pull you out of that focus. Whether you are a novice shooter or a professional, feel free to dream and to strive for your dreams, as you read and apply the strategies in this book.

But this book is more than just reading, of course. It is a specially designed high performance system based on years of training hundreds of athletes to be successful at all levels of competition, in addition to my professional education — book learning and experience — that shaped my thinking.

# Creation of a System

There was once a high performance expert who at age 10 knew there was more. Then, his target was a hockey net, and he played from sun up to sundown — full out — maniacally. It was wondrous. The outside world was nonexistent. Score seemed of no consequence but it meant everything to win the imagined cup. He enjoyed the euphoria, but never had a word for it.

But sadly, the organized version on an official ice rink — just like the organized version of any clay target discipline — threw this young expert into disarray. His game was lackluster and he could blame it on no one. Coaches, referees and opponents — who knew? But he knew the difference between his frustrating performances and his good ones, and he reveled in the rare moments — those moments of brilliance that stood out like a well-smoked target.

A fireball of energy might best have described him during those brief moments. He was skillful and unstoppable and, on a couple of occasions, there were unexpected moments where, at the end of the game, the opposing coach would pop into the locker room to praise his play. Ah, but his own coach would be rolling his eyes and sighing, as that kind of play was extremely rare for this budding high performance expert.

How had this young athlete achieved these moments of brilliance and incredible skill, endurance and awareness, when, as far as he knew then, he had done nothing different? Had he read a book on psychology? No. Had his coach suddenly turned into a grand motivator? No. Had the other team beaten up his smaller teammate and got him ripping mad? Well, yes, on one occasion. Even then the question of "how" left an indelible imprint on his brain — a mystery unsolved, a few nuggets of gold. But it was enough to start him on his quest for the mother lode.

That young man kept pursuing that dream, even at the age thirty-five — in karate. Surely, it was insight gained from maturity. He was older with an education, life experience and found himself surrounded by fabulous mentors, role models and coaches. But there he was again, the skillful athlete with no pizzazz. Something big was dragging him down, distracting him. He was being reacquainted with the "dragons" of his childhood — surely what had hampered his success as a young hockey player. He could have gone the psychology route and been assessed and talked at for hours at length. But he felt so messed up that he would have been in therapy for the rest of his life. There were tournaments around the corner and he needed a fix now.

On the verge of quitting, he began to unravel the mystery of high performance through a mix of his experience, education and luck, lots of luck. Slowly, but surely, this former perennial loser found himself using strategies that were working and helping him to win. He was succeeding in caging and/or training the dragons and, in doing so, developed a system that helped him to win a national championship in his karate organization.

## A Repeatable System

That athlete was, of course, me. And the discovery that a simple, repeatable system could be so powerful and easy to implement was very exciting. Since that time I have fine-tuned and taught my system to amateur, Olympic and professional athletes around the world, from 11-year-old aspiring trap shooters to mature ATA, American skeet, sporting clay and Olympic champions. And now I'm teaching it to you in a book designed for any age and level.

***Mind vs Target*** is designed to allow you to make sense of the system at your own shooting ability and level. As a beginner, almost everything in this book will be new and exciting and it will allow you to excel at a very rapid rate. As an advanced shooter and/or coach, you will fill in the gaps of your knowledge by understanding the tools you are already using, and, as with Paul Giambrone III, it will teach you how to use your tools much more effectively.

# Six Steps to the Zone

The SportExcel System has Six Steps to winning that, in conjunction with learning solid shooting skills, will build your mental game in everything you do, not just shooting.

## Step 1

Step 1 of the SportExcel System is the equivalent to the X Factor of television notoriety. I call it the Zone, the wonderful holy grail of sport (and life). Pick up any athlete's autobiography and you'll find a description of awesome feats of strength, playing with broken bones and uncanny anticipation, managing to slow down time, achieving perfect consistency round after round, seeing victory in the face of overwhelming odds and doing it all without thinking. The ZONE is our starting point, unlike other approaches to the mental game where the Zone is the endpoint. Making it the starting point, as you will see, makes the game a lot easier.

## Step 2

Step 2 of the SportExcel System is the outcome, also known as the prize, or goal, or the win, etc. It represents where you want to go and is the means by which you'll know if you are making progress in your game. An outcome can be any number of things, from the ideal shotgun you want, to how many targets you'll break on average.

Unlike other approaches where you write down your outcomes and read them every day, Step 2 of the SportExcel System is more about making your outcome feel doable by creating passion and excitement for it, as well as adding a touch or two of adrenaline. My findings over a decade of working with shotgunners show that anyone can quickly transform their dreams into powerful, well-adrenalized parts of THEIR LIFE, where they become Déjà Vu-like experiences. They simply feel DOABLE — and DONE — which makes them your OUTCOME!

# Step 3

Step 3 of the SportExcel System is your guidance or feedback system, and since it is similar in nature to how a GPS system in your car keeps you on track as you move to your destination, we'll call this step GPS. It is all elements of your game that you are aware of — win, lose or draw — and how you handle those elements. You'll often hear, "You'll learn more from your mistakes and losses than from your wins." Maybe; *but it's unlikely*. That will only happen if you learn the tools to help you to do that. You'll also be told to think "process" (the steps to making a great shot) rather than focus on the "outcome" (of winning), because thinking about outcome will only get you distracted or panicky or discouraged or, even, overly optimistic. Wrong. Forget it all. Step 3 of the SportExcel System will teach you how to enjoy any and all guidance so you can get to your destination every time. And it is GPS — the good, bad and ugly scores, moods, squad mates and weather – that will teach you so much. Most importantly, you'll understand the role of score in your game. I mean, let's be realistic. As I said at the outset, score is the chief reason why are you competing in your game in the first place.

## Step 4

Step 4 of the SportExcel System represents the strategies — the bulk of this book — that will help you to get back on track when distractions derail you. After so many years of being told to be confident (what is confidence?) and being told to park my bad memories (my parking lot became a piled up junk heap), I had to find another way.

Step 4 of the SportExcel System is the set of tools that will help you to forget mistakes, remove distractions, deal with difficult people, take leadership of your squad, etc. — all at the subconscious level without having to think on the stand, post, station, etc. When you have a problem, such as an agonizingly slow squad mate who is pulling you out of the Zone with his whiny voice, you'll learn to fix that problem and move on so you can shoot, not think!

## Step 5

Step 5 of the SportExcel System pulls it all together. It allows the inner workings of your mind to stay inner and working, without your external interference—often called thinking. Your subconscious mind is very capable and, once trained, can smoke any target. Your subconscious mind, *once trained*, can deal with any distraction. Your subconscious mind, once trained, can fit your clay target sport/passion/job into your life. Quite often I'll have athletes whose problems on the post or in the station are unrelated to skill, equipment or ability to get in the Zone or weather. It's work, school and other personal distractions that pop into their heads at the wrong time. "**P**- [did I forget to send that project?]-**ull**."

Step 5 of the SportExcel System will allow you to get your subconscious mind working for you to keep you focused on the task at hand.

## Step 6

Step 6 of the SportExcel System is all about you, as it is YOU who has to stick to the program. I've been there, so have hundreds of my very successful and happy athletes. Now it's your turn.

## Taking Action

So let's get started. You are about to learn the SportExcel system. It will take very little effort but lots of focused, consistent work. It will make all aspects of your game come to life — your short-term and long-term goals, your competition skills, your routines and the specific skills of your training such as gun mounts, hold points, stances, etc. This system to achieving a consistent high performance is akin to a map leading to the mother lode that prospectors dream about. As a clay target shooter, you can stop dreaming and start learning the skills required to strike it rich and win.

The SportExcel System is loaded with tools that, with consistent work, will assist you for the rest of your competitive shooting career and your life. Keep the book handy, because it is not just a one-time read. When you reach an impasse in your game or simply need a refresher, you can refer to the appropriate chapter and review the strategy. It is designed to be read — and reread.

So be prepared to ratchet up your game a notch or 20.

**High performance:** Power, focus, strength, agility, flexibility and acute perception.

**High performance:** Time slows; thoughts disappear; clay targets are predictable and larger than life; shotgun pellets find their targets by default; targets vaporize into a puff of smoke. Winning by achieving and maintaining this kind high performance is the mission of this book — your mission. Get ready, as the key to igniting the high performance Zone as a means to winning awaits you in the next chapter. So is all the new fun you'll begin having in your game.

# Step 1

## Finding Your Zone

### *Life in the Fun Lane: Igniting the Zone*

*"A mind that is stretched to a new idea never returns to its original dimensions."*
— ***Anonymous, Star Genius***

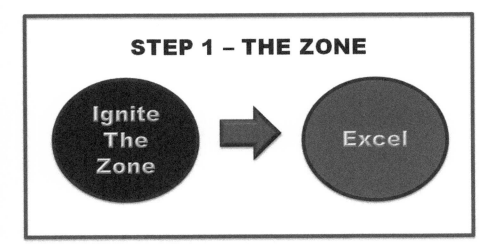

# 2   The Zone

## *What is the Zone?  Real or Mythical?*

*"The less effort, the faster and more powerful you will be."*
— **Bruce Lee, Star Actor and Martial Artist**

Immediately after my workshops, participants rush to test out their newfound tools.  They are skeptics wishing to test and verify.  And they usually surprise themselves.  Awareness is greater.  Vision is sharper.  Their guns seem light and an extension of their arms.  Targets are pulverized, not just hit.  Dropped targets seem irrelevant — just a means to readjust.  Much has changed for these shotgunners and they are now in control of their game — and smiling.  They have found the first most important component of the system, the Zone.

So what is the Zone?  Is it real or mythical?  A perfect definition of the Zone is impossible, as every athlete who has ventured into that realm has his or her own.  Based on findings from many client responses, a definition would be:

*The Zone is a sense where shooting is fun and easy, no matter what the conditions, and the targets break effortlessly* **WITH NO THINKING.** *More importantly, the Zone generates essential, ongoing agility, speed, decisiveness, strength, endurance and skillfulness.*

As for whether or not it is real, I'll leave that up to you to decide as you read this book in your quest to achieve it.

# No Secret

Achieving the Zone is less a "secret" that someone has been hiding from you all these years and more a misunderstanding by well-meaning and well-educated people. They got sidetracked by their own inability to achieve it or by their misplaced observations regarding the successful athletes who have found the Zone. I've read articles that describe the Zone as a potential detriment to success if you try too hard to achieve it before properly developing your skills. I can only shake my head at such misleading arguments.

Yet it is easy to understand how we have been misled, as the Zone often appears in random bursts of excellence that pop up willy-nilly, at bizarre moments and exits with no clues as to how to repeat it. Even the best athletes, who usually live in the Zone, are unsure of what it is exactly, as they developed it at a very early age (with no deliberate action or deep thinking). As a result, their sage advice to the rest of us can get lost in translation.

The Zone gives an incredible sense of awareness — sight, sound and feel. As a shooter, you can see the rings or dimples on the target. You can hear the minute click as the trap releases the target. You feel as though you can almost reach out with your hand and crush the target. The Zone is a pleasant and satisfying state of euphoria where the targets seem to simply break by themselves and it is all too easy.

# The Zone is a Skill

No shooting skill needs to be attached to the Zone because the Zone is a skill in itself. Beginners can feel absolutely euphoric on the shooting range or course and still miss target after target in the learning process. In so doing, however, they will learn very quickly with no frustration or discouragement. And with proper coaching, they can move through classes and become All-Americans and Master Class shooters, exercising and practicing both their shooting skill set and their Zone skill.

So, the Zone is a skill that is a pleasant and satisfying euphoria <u>within the context of a skillful game</u>. And as soon as you add that last part — the pressure of competition, dreams of being an All-American, measurement of yourself against your peers — the achievement and maintenance of the Zone becomes a lot more challenging, interesting and fun.

# Four Levels of the Zone Skill

I've come up with four arbitrary levels of the Zone Skill. The first level is simply a learning stage of *fun and play* where you have no expectations to win and the challenge is to smoke targets. The second level is where you put yourself in the position of competing against your peers. The third level is where you put yourself in a position of expecting to beat your peers. And the last level is where you KNOW the game is yours — opponents, score, weather, target quality and losing have no say in the matter — and it is all just *fun and play*.

## Skill Level One

About five years ago, I was listening to a radio interview with Mickey Rooney. He was asked what he thought was the key to his success as an actor. Rooney responded with a question of his own to the interviewer: "When did you stop being creative?" he asked. There was some stammering by the interviewer and clear irritation in his voice. "I don't think I ever lost it."

The point Rooney was trying to make was that the key to his success was his ability to play, even under the glare of cameras, retake after retake, and stay creative. Happy, creative children, own the Zone. They play, in the sandbox, with dress-up, totally absorbed in their activity.

The following are examples of a Level One Zone: Toddlers in a dance recital who are oblivious to the audience; young shooters who pick up the gun for the first time and are in total awe of the power they feel with they hit their first target; adult shooters on the practice range where there is no pressure and dropping a target has no impact on their "perfect" game.

In his book, *I Call The Shots*, golfer Johnny Miller describes his youthful prowess where he was a putting phenomenon. He notes that kids live in another world. They rely on faith, optimism and hope — and it works. But he also notes that the Zone at Stage One doesn't last long. We lose the Zone (or stop practicing it) via the pressures of life's experiences — parents, coaches or our own expectations. We learn to feel bad about being watched (put on the spot), about losing (only stupid people lose), about being put down (others are so much better than us). This, of course, sets the stage for the Level Two Zone Skill.

## Skill Level Two

Many shooters have experienced the Level Two Zone Skill. It is the kind of Zone that occurs serendipitously when you are under pressure, deadline or attack. It often happens at the height of crisis situations when you are being watched, are self-conscious or are afraid of making mistakes. You feel sick and your brow, hands and underarms are full of sweat.

And then it happens — whether it is the tone of the coach's voice, a gut reaction to a buddy having a complete meltdown or a flush of adrenaline at missing your first six targets — you get a shot of adrenaline and enter an altered state where you run targets better than ever. You feel like you can walk on water. But darn, it is fleeting and nearly impossible to get back. As hard as you work to get all the conditions that caused it, the Zone remains elusive. Sadly, not many people get beyond this stage.

## Skill Level Three

The next level is simply more of Level Two, a whole lot more. Those who get to Level Three — either because of physical ability, lots and lots of success, great role models, ability to shut themselves off from the world to practice and perfect their technique, a powerful commitment, delight in showing off, or even good genes — find themselves in the Zone on a regular basis. Since it feels euphoric and is very addicting, the athletes soon learn how to live in and know the FEEL of it. Usually, they can get the FEEL of the Zone before they start their game.

Most professional athletes are at a Level Three Zone. But it, too, is not as stable as they would like. Think of the number of really skillful athletes who only survive a year in the big leagues. Success at Level Three can be hard to maintain because it is based on the repetition of success. At this level, there is little knowledge of how they got into the Zone. Put any Level Three player on a losing team, with a negative coach, with negative teammates, with a depressed spouse, with an ADHD child, with a chronic injury — and they too will falter.

## Skill Level Four

The last and highest level of the Zone is different. It's not just a lot more of Level Three. In this case, the athletes have had their share of success as they came through Level Three, but through failure, defeat, more defeat, other adversity, luck or modeling others — they have somehow learned the tools to overcome and forget all the bad stuff. Their heads are only filled with good thoughts and fabulous outcomes.

Level Four athletes build character and retain that character. They sometimes develop late, overcome injuries, rise above difficult childhoods, create winning teams out of losing ones, thrive in problem-solving situations, etc. They never give up. They experiment all the time and make up for any physical deficits with passion, hard work and flexibility. When they get injured they figure out what it takes to come back. When they lose, they figure out what to do so it will never happen again. When they fall apart in the puff round, they train even harder for the next competition. When they feel intimidated by coaches or other athletes, they figure out how to overcome it.

One of my karate instructors was my role model for this. He would come back from losing in a competition and learn the technique that had beaten him. He would practice that technique over and over until he knew it better than his opponent. Nobody ever beat him with the same technique twice.

An amazing thing happens to athletes at a Level Four Zone. They start to play and be creative. With that creativity, they design new sets of skills that set the standard and break records. If a Level One Zone teaches us that an athlete can play and be in the Zone without skills, a Level Four Zone teaches us that an athlete can be in the Zone with skill and the game becomes play. And when you play you stay creative. Mickey Rooney had it right. To maintain your creativity, you have to learn to play.

## The Zone is Play

Play is serious business. The more seriously you strive to be playful and the more seriously you work at your game with a sense of joy and humor, the sooner your skills will allow you to pass from Level One play to Level Four play. In the next chapter I'll teach you a way to get the Zone from the get-go. It is called reverse engineering, where you'll capture the FEEL of success from past moments of brilliance and use it as a guide to extended periods of brilliance. Get ready to play!

# 3 Reverse Engineering the Zone

*How we can know before we call for the target that we will smoke it*

*"Any training that does not include the emotions, mind and body is incomplete; knowledge fades without feeling."*

**— Anonymous, Star Genius**

After a recent international event, I asked a new client what had happened during the games to keep him out of the medal round. He described all manner of distractions from faulty trap machines to a very new experience with a sizable and vocal crowd of spectators. "It affected everyone", he said. "Everyone?" I asked. "Well", he added, "Except for the eventual winner. That shooter seemed unfazed by it all." I smiled, because I had trained the winning athlete.

One had only to look at the video footage or pictures from the competition to see how clearly that athlete stood out from the field. Everything about him indicated the Zone. His posture was tall and erect and by sheer physical impact he seemed larger than his opponents. I explained this to my new client and he was intrigued, but skeptical. I smiled, as I knew that he was about to experience something he had already experienced many times previously — the Zone — only from here on in it would be on demand.

Being in the Zone is an incredible and on-going personal, exhilarating experience. Most elite athletes know the Zone. And I can assure you that you have experienced it as well, in a very clear and specific way. It was empowering to you in a shooting match or at work or in school. To others you displayed an incredible sense of confidence (and sometimes "cockiness"); you, however, may have missed what they saw. So, in this step to the Zone, you are going to:

1) Remember an experience that was successful (Zone-like),

2) Identify the feeling of it (in a specific way with a specific signal) and

3) Learn to repeat it every time you step into the station or post.

## 1) Remembering our Successes

We all have a wealth of great experiences in shooting and/or in other areas of our lives. Thinking of these experiences as the Zone is unfamiliar territory — a few shots here, a few rounds there, perhaps an unexpected day of pure joy. I have yet to find anyone who is so perfectly awful that they consistently miss. You have moments, and you may need to search your mind to find them, but these are your moments of brilliance — they are your starting point. These experiences, believe it or not, are you in the Zone. The stronger your memory of these events — with sight, sound and feeling — the more powerful they will be in terms of helping you to identify your Zone.

## 2) Identifying Your Zone

Next we want to identify your Zone specifically — as it will give you a precise way of knowing if you are in it before you step anywhere near the range. It is relatively easy to identify someone else's Zone and whether he or she is going to shoot well — there's a level of focus, calm attention and certainty. There's the posture and solid stance. There is the solid gaze. It is relatively easy for others to see it in you — but, unfortunately, there is no mirror you can hold up in front of yourself as you shoot. Nor can you have a coach perched on your shoulder to remind you that you are in the Zone or not. Nor can you guide yourself with self-talk. The first two are silly, the last requires thinking.

We need another way, one that is truly obvious to us. So we'll use your sense of feel, similar to the sensation you feel when a sneeze is building up inside you. This Zone FEEL will be evident and as clear as a traffic signal where you know when to enter an intersection, a camcorder recording light when you are video recording successfully or the ding of an egg timer when it is time to eat a perfectly cooked egg. If you want a repeatable Zone, you will require an identifiable signal, a sensation that is clear and unmistakable just as these three.

Elite athletes develop this "sweet-spot" feeling over time through success, diligent work on their game or sheer luck. Somehow the rest of us missed out, so we need to develop our own sweet spot now, by taking stock of our past successes and noticing what they tell us. That is where our moments of brilliance come in, however great or insignificant they may have appeared to you. Whether your moment came in clay target shooting or in another sport, your task now is to identify that this event had a specific identifiable FEEL that you missed or downplayed the first go round.

## 3) Repeatable Zone

Your telltale feeling in your moment of brilliance is the biggest gift your body has ever given you. You are going to re-experience that feeling, learn to get it back on demand and then experience how it brings out your best performance. This is essentially *reverse engineering* and, when you trust it, it will give you a repeatable Zone:

**When I was in the Zone, I got a feeling.**

**Now when I get the feeling, I know I'm in the Zone**

Let's find out how it works.

## Exercise: Find Your Zone FEEL

**a) Take a moment to think about one of your moments of brilliance (MOB).** What were you doing? What did you see in that moment? What did you hear? How did your body feel? What were you doing physically when you were shooting effortlessly, easily? To the best of your ability, see, hear and feel this experience. As you relive this memory, "go inside" your body and notice your breathing pattern. Is it full and even? Notice the feeling of your posture. Is it upright? Notice your muscles and any other internal sensations in your chest, abdomen or limbs. Make a list of the sensations as demonstrated in the following chart.

| 1st Moment of Brilliance | 2nd Moment of Brilliance | 3rd Moment of Brilliance |
|---|---|---|
| **Examples:**<br>☑ Breathing is faster<br>☑ Posture more erect<br>☑ Arms and hands light<br>☑ Chest expansive<br>☑ Electricity in chest<br>☑ Abdomen feels solid | | |

**b) Repeat step 1 of this exercise for two more MOBs.** Similarly make a list of the sensations.

**c) Now compare your lists.** You are looking for *one sensation that is similar* from experience to experience. Personally, when I'm in the Zone, I feel energy (an electric feeling) in my chest. Clients I've worked with all have their own unique sensations, such as tingling in their fingertips, warmth in their abdomen or a relaxed neck. The *ONE* sensation you choose is your own, so be sure that it is strong and clear and identifiable. Remember the ding of the egg timer — unmistakable.

**d) Now close your eyes and identify that sensation in your body.** Notice what happens to your ability to focus, to your sense of being at your best. Intensify the sensation and see how it makes you feel. This sensation, as you'll discover, will create greater focus and a general sense of being unstoppable on the range. If that's your sense, it is now up to you to take it to your range (or the office or school) and to experience how well it holds up.

And that is Zone FEEL — the most important piece of equipment in your arsenal to date. So ask yourself: "If I feel this the next time I step on the range or course, how will I shoot?" It is you at your best; trust what it is telling you.

## Chapter Summary

By learning to identify your Zone FEEL, by calling it up on demand and by using it every time you shoot, you will transform your shooting game. It tells you that you are running optimally right from the get-go. Learn to identify and KNOW this feeling. It is your entry point for the Zone and the real fun will be to maintain it in the face of fierce competition, lousy weather, wonky trap machines, long tiring days, irritable people and travel. Get used to it; trust it, because there will be days when it is hard to get into or sustain. And those days will be gut wrenching — a feeling that is the equally important dark side of the Zone of the next chapter. Read on.

# 4 Feeling Bad is Good

*How shooting poorly can teach you so much*

*"In great attempts it is glorious even to fail."*

**— Vince Lombardi, Star Football Coach**

When I think back to my competitive years in the martial arts, I had my share of really enjoyable successes but I also had my share of incredibly fabulous losses — yes, fabulous losses. This notion that losses can be useful and that there are benefits to losing, often sparks disbelief. How could losing and feeling bad be good? As much as I enjoyed winning — and it was the only reason I was in the game in the first place — losing forced me into many difficult corners that I had to fight my way out of. Each corner proved to be an incredible opportunity to get fed up and quit — or, fight through it and, in the process, develop physical skills, realign mental strategies and test my commitment to my sport.

I know you are probably tired of hearing that you learn much more from losing than winning. So, instead of leaving you hanging with this advice, I'm going to teach you to get very excited when you lose so that you can wring every last drop out of what it is teaching you.

You have now developed your internal signal or Zone FEEL that boldly indicates that you are prepared for battle. With Zone FEEL, there is one and only one thing you notice — the feeling that you can hit any target, anywhere, anytime. In this chapter, I'm going coin a term — NO Zone — to describe when you fall out of the Zone. With the corresponding NO-Zone FEEL, there is an awareness of sensations that are distinctly opposite and perhaps unpleasant. And there may be many things jumbled in your mind as you are starting to think!

All Olympic-level shotgunners I've worked with have experienced NO-Zone situations where they are smoking targets one round and chipping or missing them the next. In one case, an Olympian described a round where she chipped two targets right at the start of the round. What had happened to cause her to momentarily lose her Zone? She wasn't sure, as the only thing she could think of was a teammate saying, "You'll love the targets; I did." Now the comment seems benign (and why it affected her will become apparent in Chapter 18), but she felt the shift in her Zone and had to take corrective action.

Most of us can find that same NO Zone in a heartbeat — our slumped shoulders and frown lines giving us away — as well as the dropped targets. Some of us are in the NO Zone most of the time and walk around with a cloud over our heads. Worse yet, most of us have no knowledge of what causes it. We have lots of excuses, of course, and you can hear them on the range every day, everything from wind to cranky squad mates. That is why, just as we have a useful signal for the Zone, we need an indicator for the NO Zone: a clear NO-Zone feeling telling us that — oops — we need to take action or we'll end up in a very unpleasant downward spiral.

# Finding Your NO Zone

Most of us have clearly evident NO-Zone sensations that we usually describe as embarrassment, anger, depression, frustration, etc. But we are more interested in the associated unpleasant internal sensations — butterflies, nausea, difficulty breathing, sweaty palms, heaviness — that reveal just as much as our Zone FEEL — because they are a warning. Yes, they give you a heads-up. And if you can anticipate disaster, you can avoid it. So, just as in the last chapter I had you think of past experiences that "reverse engineered" your Zone, you are going to apply the same process to find a sensation for your NO Zone — a NO-Zone FEEL — so you can KNOW when you are in danger of going over the cliff and can pull back from the brink.

# Exercise: The NO-Zone FEEL

1) **Take a moment to think about a moment of disaster (MOD), one where you were angry or frustrated, for example, at your inability to be consistent.** What were you doing? What did you see in that moment? What did you hear? What did you feel physically when this happened? To the best of your ability, see, hear and feel this experience. As you relive this memory, "go inside" and notice your breathing pattern. Is it restricted? Notice your posture. Is it a bit slumped? Notice your muscles and any other internal sensations in your chest, abdomen or limbs. Make a list of the sensations as demonstrated in the following chart.

| 1st Moment of Disaster | 2nd Moment of Disaster | 3rd Moment of Disaster |
|---|---|---|
| **Examples:**<br>☑ Breathing is tight<br>☑ Posture is slumped<br>☑ Arms and hands heavy<br>☑ Chest hollow<br>☑ Butterflies in stomach<br>☑ Chest contracted | | |

**2) Repeat step 1 of this exercise for two more MODs.** Similarly make a list of the sensations.

**3) Now compare the experiences.** You are looking for *one sensation* that is similar across all of your moments of disaster. Personally, I feel sick to my stomach (tight with butterflies). Clients I've worked with have their own unique sensations, such as leaden arms, hollow chest, hot face or stiff neck. The *ONE* NO-Zone FEEL you choose is your own personal signal, so be sure it is strong, clear and identifiable.

**4) Now, close your eyes and identify that sensation in your body.** Notice what happens to your focus. Ask yourself: "If I feel like this when I step into the post or station, how will I shoot?" If the answer is: "Terrible," then you are in good company as this represents a very similar sensation to what everyone who loses the Zone feels. This is a very important signal — a warning to fix some part of your game.

# Develop your NO-Zone FEEL

By developing awareness of your NO-Zone FEEL, you will now be able to identify problems with your shooting before they result in missed targets. As soon as you feel it, you will say, "aha," I know what is happening. It was the person who just said *that* to me. It was *me* watching the other shooter drop a target. It was *me* listening to my squad mate's whiny call for the target. Now your NO-Zone FEEL is the means by which you identify and take corrective action *before* you miss. The Olympic shooter knew that she needed to take action by her NO-Zone FEEL, even though she missed the original comment that caused it.

Now, even in the pressure of a competition, instead of thinking, "Oh no, here we go again," you too will become adept at shifting quickly back to your Zone. It will tell you much about how the Zone and NO Zone affects your body and your game. And, of course, by the time you finish this book, you will have the tools to correct the NO-Zone FEEL, by employing a wealth of strategies.

# Chapter Summary

Get used to the No-Zone FEEL. Become aware of it. Trust it. You need it to be so blatantly obvious that you'll feel as sheepish for missing it in your game, as you would for getting ticketed for missing a red light. It will soon help you to learn from your mistakes and losses and allow you to have a spectacular guidance system on the road to excellence.

In the next chapter, we'll move on to Step 2 — your goals turned into outcomes — and fully accept that the reason for needing a system in the first place — to learn how to win.

Know and practice your Zone and No-Zone signals before reading on!

# Step 2

---

## Outcomes Alive

*Only losers say: "It's only a game."*

*"Everything is practice."*

**— Pele, Star Soccer Player**

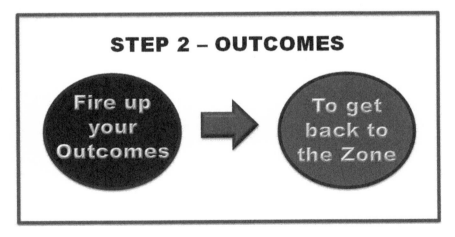

# 5     Turning Goals into a Done Deal

*I write them down, read them every day and then lose the list.*

*"Don't think about winning. Think about dominating!"*

**— Pierre Pryor, Star Wrestler and Coach**

Within the shooting sports there are notable shotgunners always in the shoot-offs. Somehow they learned to be consistent by way of incredible talent, many hours of training and many hours fighting through vast numbers of competition targets. So you ask yourself, can I ever catch up and become as good as they are? And can I possibly do it sooner rather than later? Most things being equal (equipment, coaching and range time), in this chapter I am going to show you how you can begin to equal the playing field by putting in extra practice time and competing in hundreds of additional tournaments — at no cost and minimal time — just by processing your goals a bit differently and seeing them as "done deals" or outcomes.

This is Step 2 of the SportExcel System for high performance. You are going to go on a training regimen where much of your training will be done in your head through a process I call DÉJÀ VU, because shooters who have won many times over KNOW they'll do it again — no thinking, no doubt. And you need to be just like them when you compete — no thinking, no doubt.

With DÉJÀ VU, you will experience your outcome of winning just like Master Class, World Champion or All-American shooters do. When your success starts with such a strong sense of KNOWING, it'll feel like a foregone conclusion.

# DÉJÀ VU Guidelines

The DÉJÀ VU Strategy uses what is often called visualization or guided imagery or game rehearsal. But there is more — a very obvious physical component that is so subtle you sometimes miss it. But you'll feel it. And, when you do it properly, you'll feel like you are on the range where the targets are in living color and the smell of gun powder is real and you'll be "at one" with the shotgun and be able to crush the target. Oh, and you'll get to experience what it feels like to be on the podium.

Most importantly, you'll actually feel micro-muscle movements, a process that I've coined "physicalization," based on some work I've done with Olympic athletes who feel in their rehearsal exactly the same way they feel in competition. The ultimate aim with visualization and physicalization is to rehearse your goals so precisely that you begin to feel that you have already been to the competition, got the T-shirt and WON. Hence, DÉJÀ VU .

Here are the rules of "DÉJÀ VU -ing":

**1) Know what you want.** What does winning mean to you? Will you be on the podium? Or will you be in the top five, 10 or other? Will you punch up a level? Know these things and the resulting DEJA-VU practice session will be easy, precise and empowering. And remember to include the podium or victory dance or celebration. It is why you participate in sport, end of story.

**2) Be engaged.** A while ago I was working with a young skier who was reluctant to follow the DÉJÀ-VU process (or anything I said), mostly because his coach had taught him another way. I asked him to take a moment and visualize his most recent race as an example. He closed his eyes for several seconds and when he reopened them, I told him that he had crashed. He looked at me wide-eyed as if to say, how did you know? I knew because he went from sitting upright in the chair to being slightly slumped. His body said it all; it was disengaged from his mind.

How you practice the DÉJÀ-VU Strategy is how you will perform, fully engaged, or not. In Chapter 22, I'll discuss the importance of managing your adrenaline levels so that you can have a steady supply at the start and throughout the competition. In the meantime, you'll need to get acquainted with your adrenaline so that you can use some in your DÉJÀ-VU practice session, before you get anywhere near the range.

**3) Have the feeling of having been there many times before.** The more often you do DÉJÀ-VU practice, the more comfortable you will get in competition. I used DÉJÀ-VU to help me rehearse for my black belt tournaments in the kata, or forms component, which is a combination of dance, fighting technique, bar brawl, athleticism and over-the-top energy.

Before utilizing this approach, the smallest mistakes in my form, perhaps not even discernible to the judges, would get me thinking and trigger the NO Zone. A mere eight weeks later in the ring — which is plenty of time to rehearse the Zone using DÉJÀ-VU but not enough to correct all imperfections — the head judge was in front of me flipping his score cards with the same intensity that I had displayed in the ring. I was in the Zone, and he'd felt it. I'd surely made some mistakes; yet I got the highest score I'd ever received. Eight weeks, seven days each week, three times a day — I'd won that event more than 168 times and it was a moment that nothing could derail.

**4) DÉJÀ VU is a skill-building process, where you build skills in both your technique and your general performance.** While this kind of rehearsal is not a substitute for having a shotgun in your hand and real targets flying across the sky, it greatly enhances regular practice and in many cases it will help you to resolve flaws in routines or to practice in conditions that might be hard to create, such as windstorms or torrid heat. You can also save huge sums by smoking imaginary targets with imaginary shells. More importantly, what you learn in competition can be applied to your Déjà Vu practice so that you can continually narrow the gap between what you want and where you currently are in your sport.

## Exercise: DÉJÀ-VU DVD

DÉJÀ-VU DVD takes advantage of the brain's incredible capacity to rehearse an upcoming event, both visually and physically. As you do this exercise, understand that your idea of visualization may be quite different from your squad mates'. Some will see images in living color, some will see hazy shades of black and white and some see absolutely nothing, even though they seem to know exactly what they are viewing.

## Step 1: Visualization.

a) Sit in a comfortable chair in a room away from distractions.

b) Close your eyes and see a DVD player and TV in front of you. In your hand, you hold the DVD of your upcoming competition. The name of the event and the date are transcribed in bold letters on the disk. This is a recording of your future. Insert the disk into the imaginary DVD player and turn on the TV. As you watch your performance in your mind, be amazed by your incredible skill and poise. Note how much fun you are having. Sit on the edge of your seat as you watch and feel your adrenaline and Zone FEEL.

c) Watch the entire event, the joys of the hits and especially the amazing recovery after your misses. Play the DVD for as long as you like.

## Step 2: Physicalization

a)   Now, in your mind, step up into your image on the screen, so that you become the person you've been watching. From this vantage point, notice all the people around you, from competitors to officials. Then step into the station or post, go through all your routines, call for the target and smoke it.

b)   Continue with your round, station to station or post to post, and experience your Zone FEEL. You feel the adrenaline; targets evaporate into puffs of smoke. Enjoy.

c)   Step off the screen, remove the DVD and note the date on it. This is your future. Place the DVD in your "back pocket" and pull it out daily to watch and rehearse your success.

And that is it — short and sweet — or as long as you want to make it. I encourage you to do DÉJÀ-VU DVD practice at least once a day — both the visualization and the physicalization components. If you practice in the evening, there may come a time when your adrenaline will kick in so quickly and powerfully that you may find getting to sleep difficult afterward. At this point, reschedule DÉJÀ-VU DVD practice to the morning or afternoon.

# Chapter Summary

Using DÉJÀ-VU DVD gives you the same advantage all elite shotgunners have. They know that they are going to win before they get anywhere near the range. The exercise enables you to rehearse both your skills and your Zone. At the outset, ensure you have a quiet place to watch your DVD. After a while, you'll find the training effective even in noisy airport waiting areas and on the plane itself.

Watch your DVD and enjoy the feeling of confidence it gives you. Become the high performance champion of your dreams in the comfort of your own chair. You'll save time, save money and learn to hit the targets hard. In the next chapter, we'll look at an example of how the DÉJÀ-VU DVD strategy is used in a sport situation.

# 6 Creating Déjà Vu Requires Practice

*Mental rehearsal and physical rehearsal are opposite sides of the same coin*

*"You cannot discover new oceans unless you have the courage to lose sight of the other shore."*

*— Anonymous, Star Genius*

From karate to the clay target sports, using DÉJÀ-VU DVD in Step 2 of this system helps you acquire and fine-tune skills to compete at the highest levels. Because I've also worked with several other sports, I'll give you an example of the DÉJÀ-VU DVD process from the point of view of learning a sport far removed from shooting clay targets — snowboarding. It will give you a sense of how you can accelerate your learning curve and practice crushing clay targets in your head as opposed to on the range.

I have always enjoyed skiing without being competitive and without having to imagine being a high performance racer. However, a friend observed me skiing and said I had all the balance and finesse of a hockey player who needed something to hit. It was, she said, the kind of finesse that classy skiers avoided being associated with (partly for safety reasons).

However, she agreed to swallow her pride and teach me some of the finer points.

Over the next two skiing seasons, she encouraged me to "step into her shoes" and model her style and technique as I followed her down the hill. She gave me specific pointers and showed me how to plant my ski poles, which, up to then, had been only useful, I thought, for skewering fellow skiers as I awkwardly got on or off the lift. At times I felt fabulous, at times scared, and most of the time I felt like I was going way too fast. So, on the many trips up the lift, I visualized and physicalized competent athletic sweeps across and down the hill.

Knowing that I was a karate instructor, my friend turned the tables on me and gave me levels of success — yellow belt to start and progressing upward — grading me like I grade my karate students. I liked and understood that and it gave me an outcome to strive for. Eventually, two years from that first lesson, I started to feel comfortable and a little classy myself — perhaps a skiing brown belt — as my speeds were faster but felt slower. So I was not prepared when she cornered me on the lift and said, in a matter of fact, not to be argued with voice: "Let's take up snowboarding next year."

My heart nearly stopped. "Are you crazy?" I wanted to say. But, being male, I said, "Sure, why not?"

Ouch. My backside already began to hurt just thinking about snowboarding. I even plugged the thought into a DÉJÀ-VU DVD and my initial attempts made me feel queasy and produced a disquieting array of images of bumping down the hill, slinky-like, mostly on my backside, sometimes on my head. I'd never really felt panic before with sports, not even in karate. Snowboarding was different. My DVD of being strapped to a "plank," helmeted and wrist splinted, and going headlong down a mountain felt like suicide.

My saving grace, I suppose, is the career that I follow and my ability to walk my talk. If I can get athletes to overcome fear, I thought, I can do it for myself — I hoped. I'd watched a lot of snowboarding at the winter Olympics in 2010 — keeping tabs on a talented young athlete with whom I'd worked — so I had amazing snowboarding images in my head — the world's best, for example, Shaun White. I went back to the DÉJÀ-VU DVD process and pretended to be him. I had my doubts (probably because of my allergy to pain) but within about five minutes of DÉJÀ-VU DVD practice I was able to imagine myself sweeping across the hill. It was cool.

Taking it to the next level, I attempted to carve (which means to weave gracefully back and forth in an S pattern), but that still eluded me and evoked the queasiness. And that's where I sit as I write this. However, I'm persisting. And each day I practice DÉJÀ VU, I expect the queasiness to grow fainter. My goal is to practice in this way over the entire summer, so that when winter comes and I am strapped into a snowboard, my progress will be effortless and, more importantly, painless!

## Exercise: DÉJÀ-VU Two

As I'm discovering, no sport or aspect of a sport is too complicated (or scary) for the DÉJÀ-VU DVD process. Give it a try yourself in your clay target game and experiment with the following exercise.

**1) Start by feeling adrenaline surging in your veins**, and, of course, experience your Zone FEEL.

**2) With the adrenalized sensation, visualize yourself in a shoot-off.** See yourself in the station or post, larger than life, calmer than calm, outrageously competent, smoking target after target. (I like to see myself 10' tall.)

**3) Now, make the experience physical — shot after shot.** This IS training so have yourself miss the occasional target just so you can see yourself overcoming anything — wind, rain, wonky trap machines — without missing a beat. Put yourself in all kinds of conditions — hot and cold — just to get your body and brain used to what you may face in competition.

**4) Next, take it a step further** and (just as I challenged myself in snowboarding) transform the difficult parts of your shooting by seeing yourself as comparable to the All-American or Master Class shotgunners you have ever seen — one, two or even 20 different shotgunners — until it feels good to go toe-to-toe with them and you have the Zone FEEL all the while you do it.

Shotgunners participate in an expensive sport, so it makes sense to use DÉJÀ-VU DVD to elevate your game in a shorter time with less expense. Visualizing *is* practice, and it not only helps you get started as a beginner, it helps shotgunners at all levels to build confidence and consistency and overcome any number of problematic parts of their game. You already have many images of excellence in your head. Utilize them and make DÉJÀ-VU practice a daily part of your practice regimen, especially before on-range training sessions and competitions

## Chapter Summary

My snowboarding DÉJÀ-VU practice will eventually be put to the test, and my current anxiety level reveals a lot more work still needs to be done. However, when you know your outcome and know beforehand what it will look and feel like, you'll have a much greater chance of getting it done. Any way you look at it, the quest for the Zone starts with your ability to get excited by your future. In the next chapter we'll set up some parameters around DÉJÀ-VU DVD practice to further enhance your chances of winning.

# 7 More Than Just Winning!

---

*Winning is a nice way of living life to the fullest; so is having friends.  Both can be mutually inclusive.*

"Love the game. Love the game for the pure joy of accomplishment.

Love the game for everything it can teach you about yourself.

Love the game for the feeling of belonging to a group endeavoring to do its best.

Love the game for being involved in a team whose members can't wait to see you do your best. Love the game for the challenge of working harder than you ever have at something and then harder than that.

Love the game because it takes all team members to give it life.

Love the game because at its best, the game tradition will include your contributions.

Love the game because you belong to a long line of fine athletes who have loved it. It is now your legacy.

Love the game so much that you will pass on your love of the game to another athlete who has seen your dedication, your work, your challenges, your triumphs... and then that athlete will, because of you, love the game."

**— Anonymous, Star Motivator**

Several years ago, I was working with a young athlete who had an awful experience at a major U.S. event. He is a very capable shotgunner and especially adept at using what his coaches and my system have taught him. But in a session before a major competition, he had told me he was going to win for his family and community, as they had been helping him raise money for his training. I almost stopped him on the spot so he could further explain this outcome, but I held my tongue. I figured it would be a good experience for him to discover how being focused on the wrong outcome might be counterproductive. For example, one can set the goal to be rich, but, if this is done by robbing banks, there will be a problem.

## Careful what you wish for

Being totally focused on the outcome of winning — for love or money — is fraught with similar pitfalls. It can become an unhealthy obsession that may blind us to problematic behaviors. It can also obscure the ethical side of sport where performance-enhancing drugs may appear justified. And it can create a "win at all costs" mentality by which other deviousness gets played out.

To this end, I have witnessed karate instructors cheating — but not by conscious choice or bad character. In my style of karate, where instructors will occasionally be part of a panel that judges their own students, some judges will see or miss obvious points that favor their own students. I believe they had no *conscious* intent to cheat. But, based on their very powerful outcomes of wanting their own athlete to win, only the points their athletes scored could fit that outcome.

Just as I teach athletes to make distractions such as wind and rain "disappear" in order to stay in the Zone, these same instructors make some athletes' points — "mere distractions" — disappear as well. If I were to accuse these instructors of playing favorites, they would be defensive and appalled. Quite simply, these instructors have muddied their outcomes. The outcome they set of helping their students prepare for and win the competition meshes rather poorly with judging these same students against their opponents.

Coaches get caught in another trap as well. Sometimes they will play favorites with their own athletes, especially those who are most fulfilling to work with. And it makes sense. These athletes learn the fastest, take on responsibility and leadership and make the coach look good by winning. Hence, they will often get most of the coach's attention (even though the coach may not be aware of this). Coaches who get caught in this trap can even unintentionally undermine the rest of their athletes. Once again, I believe that most coaches would be in denial and be truly appalled if this were pointed out to them.

Going for the win as an athlete has similar pitfalls. Golfers who cheat and get caught may refuse to acknowledge their behavior. Even if the illegal act were caught on camera, they may be unable to see the error of their ways. When you set the outcome to win, it gets wired in, the subconscious mind takes over and strange things can happen. People who never cheat will cheat, and they are hard-pressed to be convinced that they did wrong because they have been raised in good homes where cheating is something only bad guys do.

The young athlete I mentioned earlier had a different problem with his outcome of winning — called losing. He loved his parents and community sponsors and greatly appreciated their financial support in his quest for success. He believed that winning honored their support and, by default, losing dishonored it. What an incredible burden for any athlete to carry.

I can think of many athletes who have won world championships and then faltered in an Olympic year when their country's honor was at stake. (Some athletes, of course, do just the opposite.) The national audience is watching for the first time and there is an ongoing tally of the country's self-worth as measured by the medals. "The Russians and Chinese are nipping on our heels." With the country's honor at stake, and dad and mom watching, the athlete may find this burden difficult to bear.

I've been asked, "Isn't going for the prize and the glory everyone's outcome?" Of course it is — but that's only a part of it. There are a wealth of other components that can give perspective and balance. There has to be, or why would so many shotgunners bother to come back year after year to the competitions when there are only a few winners?

When setting outcomes for competitions, I encourage athletes to start with their dream of winning the big prize. Then I get them to enrich the experience by stepping back and creating sub-outcomes that will ultimately support that dream. I ask one simple question of every shotgunner: "If you were to have fun and be in the Zone for the whole competition, how would you do?" The answer is usually "I'd do well." This is the first complementary outcome to winning: *Stay in the Zone.*

# Sub-Outcomes for Success

There are five sub-outcomes for you when you are heading to a competition. When you can succeed in all five, you will be learning how to support the main outcome of winning and have a great experience as a bonus.

**1) Establish and learn Zone FEEL.** You have already learned this. If not, go back to Chapter 3. It IS that important.

**2) Get excited by mistakes, losses and emotional collapses.** They will happen, so you might as well learn from them. Competitions give you an incredible opportunity to learn and improve your game by fixing the fallout. By the time you finish this book you will have quite the tool kit with which to do this.

**3) Act on everything that happens to you.** It is all good. In Step 3 of the SportExcel System we'll develop this further, as each time you make any correction or fix any problem, it goes into your mental data bank and builds the resolute, competitive skills that go beyond your conscious mind. In my years of martial arts competition I ultimately learned more from my losses than I did from my victories. (I did appreciate my victories however. They were sweet.)

**4) Perceive the world as a friendly place where everything works to your advantage.** When it is windy, you love wind. When it is rainy, you love rain. When the officials are cranky, you love to get them on your side. When you have to shoot against the best shooters in the county, state, province, country or world, you love the challenge and any attempts to intimidate you.

**5) Enjoy the friends and coaches you meet at competitions.** An "osmosis" learning effect takes place here: what you learn from these relationships cannot be taught on the practice range. You also can enjoy the exotic locations, travel, opportunity to represent your club, town, or country, the scenery and the mementoes. These experiences will make you a better shooter, create memories that will last a lifetime and keep you coming back.


# Chapter Summary

When you flesh out your "outcome to win" with the five sub-outcomes you will continue to grow in your abilities; you will make incredible life-long coaching and competitive allies; you will be well-respected outside of competition and feared within it; you will become a student of the game; and you will honor everyone who knows you. It is also the path to consistency and achieving your dream of winning. By setting up proper outcomes in Step 2, you will learn the path to the Zone in all aspects of competition — AND I BELIEVE YOU WILL ULTIMATELY HAVE A MUCH GREATER CHANCE OF WINNING. In the next chapter, I'll encourage you to keep your outcomes very specific.

# 8 Covering all of the Bases

*Now that you're wildly excited about the prospects for the new season, you'll need to dig a little deeper and work on specifics*

*"Nothing is particularly hard if you divide it into small jobs."*

**— Henry Ford, Star Entrepreneur**

As you approach any new season, you'll be excitedly gnawing on the bit with all manner of possibilities for the shooting adventure that lies ahead. You'll be rested, having taken some time off to recover from a year of competitions. Shooters in snowy northern climes are forced to take a break, but it is crucial for everyone to have a rest, whether your previous year was wildly successful, or not. But with the hibernation over, this is the point in the season, before any targets are smoked or missed, to set your specific outcomes for the year. When you project what you want to achieve — in a checklist fashion — you'll know month by month if you are achieving them and making any progress in your game.

Aw, you might say, but I'm only a recreational shooter and setting specific outcomes makes recreational shooting sound like work. Well, it is, and it does, but only at the beginning of the season. Once you get into full stride, it'll make your season easier. That is because setting your own outcomes puts the responsibility in your hands. Here is the choice:

1) You can have your colleagues—some who may be very negative and disruptive — set outcomes for you;

2) You can allow your subconscious mind — with all its negative self-talk and minor phobias — to set outcomes for you; or

3) You can be the one to set them consciously. Outcomes are going to happen and it is just a matter of how, and by whom, they get set.

When I was a young athlete I set no outcomes, not consciously at least, although I knew I was going to play hockey in the National Hockey League. For me, the only other goal I knew had mesh, was framed in steel, and was where I had to get the puck. Even as a high school football player, I set no outcomes. In recreational sports such as tennis, squash, badminton and table tennis, I set no outcomes. Karate, as I remember it, was the only sport where I set outcomes, but the sport was laid out in an outcome-oriented progression of belt levels. For tournaments, however, my outcomes were about not losing, versus what I really wanted, winning. As I mentioned earlier, I changed that around pretty quickly with the DÉJÀ-VU DVD exercise.

If this sways you to get serious about outcome setting, the first thing you need to do is to specifically define your outcomes for the year. You need to write down your outcomes as you want them to unfold as part of a training plan in technique training, physical training (which includes healthy eating, mental training and tournament experience).

If this sounds like a plan for an Olympic development team, it is, but it is also for you. Pat Laib, a competitive shooter from Minnesota, told me setting outcomes was the best thing he could have done as this allowed him to know exactly how many registered targets he needed over the course of the season and when to schedule them.

The process is straightforward and can produce incredible results, both in your shooting and in your life. Outcomes such as walking a few times a week, losing thirty pounds and striving to be happier or more pleasant can certainly improve your stamina over a couple of days of shooting, help you to feel better and, perhaps, get your spouse and family to sit up and take notice.

Outcomes such as improving your technique can introduce you to some incredible coaches who have years of experience and a wealth of strategies. Outcomes such as improving your mental game can give you a personal calmness and consistency and ability to bring out the best in yourself. And outcomes such as enjoying competition can build a sense of wellbeing like nothing you can imagine. So, set out outcomes for your competitive year in these categories — physical training, technical training, mental training and competing — then find the resources to support this training.

# Physical Training

The physical training will involve anything from walking to jogging to running to cycling to swimming, to name a few. Of course, take into consideration the normal disclaimer that you need to consult your physician if you are starting from scratch or have weight or health challenges. Be specific as to how much exercise you are going to do and write the times on a weekly schedule. Start with fewer reps and move to greater ones. Set your outcomes so your workout follows a plan and is time limited. That way you won't quit early — unless you feel ill — and, and you won't extend it, even if you feel fantastic. Set it up in this way and you'll find a greater success staying committed to your outcome.

# Technical Training

Technical training should involve a coach so that you have a shooting system and a way of getting guidance on your technique. Otherwise, you may be rehearsing, over and over, using wrong technique in a very technical game such as shooting. With your practice outcomes, set the amount of time and lay out a plan for your training. Ask your coach to give you specific drills. Write out your plan and go from drill to drill, ending with a competition style round or some other fun activity. Stick with your plan and stick with your time allotment. Completing your plan sets you up for success. Pat yourself on the back. Learn to enjoy success.

# Mental Training

Your mental training is ongoing and continues throughout your physical training, technical training and competing. Set outcomes around the amount of time you will spend on this. They say that sport is 90 per cent mental and 10 per cent physical, but you'd never spend 90 per cent of your time training mentally as it can be boring. However, you can invert the ratio and spend 10 per cent on mental training and 90 per cent on physical and technical training as the mind can compress a whole lot of mental practice into a short period of time. In five minutes of mental work, you can shoot 100 targets, very effectively and very cheaply. The exercises I'm presenting in the following chapters can very easily give you plenty of mental work to do, but you may also benefit from additional tools from a high performance expert.

## Competition Training

Lastly, you want to craft some outcomes around how you want to compete. Competing involves a whole different skill set and a whole different set of outcomes to support it. You need to be able to respond to efforts to undermine or intimidate you. You need to love putting yourself on the line and treat competition like a friend. You need to be flexible and to be able to recover quickly from mistakes. You need to know how much time you expect to stay in the Zone and where you will finish on the leader board. It is important to spend some time setting these kinds of outcomes as all the practice and all the technical skill in the world can come to naught under the spotlight of competition.

## Mileposts with the scorecard

Of course, all of these areas need to be evaluated from time to time over your shooting season and modified if necessary or changed as you complete your outcomes, but you have to write them down at the outset. So I've provided a very simple example of a countdown chart that you can use as a template to create your own chart on a single sheet of paper or on the computer. At a glance you'll be able to see how your year will unfold, starting with the year-end month AT THE TOP and working downward to the start of your year AT THE BOTTOM. This may seem odd to you but I encourage you to do it this way so that the first thing you always see is where you want to get to by the end of your season. It is nice, neat and tidy and at a glance you can see the path you are going to take. And, when an outcome is completed, you check it off. So, if you haven't already done so, set your outcomes for your season now — even if the season has already started.

| Month | Example of Countdown Chart Outcomes | ✓ |
|---|---|---|
| **Sept** <br> (The end of your season) | Final Competition of year shoot 95 or better — live in the Zone <br> Daily walking and exercise — lose 30 pounds, Visualization daily <br> Practice at range with coach X times <br> Only eat healthy foods, Technique well-oiled and smooth | |
| **Aug** | 6th competition -- 95 or better (year goal 95 or better) live in Zone <br> Daily walking and exercise Increase — lose 27 of 30 pounds <br> Visualization daily, Maintain gun mounts <br> Practice at range with coach X times eating | |
| **July** | 5th competition -- 90 or better (year goal 95 or better) (have fun) <br> Daily walking and exercise — lose 24 of 30 pounds — healthy eating <br> Visualization daily, Maintain gun mounts <br> Practice at range with coach X times | |
| **June** | 4th competition -- 90 or better (year goal 95 or better) (have fun) <br> Daily walking and maintain exercise — lose 21 of 30 pounds — only healthy eating choices, Visualization daily <br> Maintain gun mounts, Practice at range with coach X times | |
| **May** | 3rd competition -- 85 or better (year goal 95) (have fun) <br> Daily walking and maintain exercise — lose 18 of 30 pounds — only healthy eating choices, Visualization daily <br> Maintain gun mounts, Practice at range with coach X times | |
| **April** | 2nd competition — set new standard or goal or 85 or better (have fun) <br> Daily walking and maintain exercise — lose 15 of 30 pounds — consistent healthy eating choices. Visualization daily, Maintain gun mounts <br> Practice at range with coach X times | |
| **March** | 1st competition (have fun, ignore score) <br> Daily walking and increase exercise — lose 12 of 30 pounds — consistent healthy eating choices, Increase visualization to daily <br> Reduce gun mounts , Dry firing replaced by practice along and with coach | |
| **Feb** | Practice on shooting range — relax have fun – obtain services of coach <br> Maintain visualization, 3x weekly flashlight drill <br> Maintain Gun Mounts, Maintain walking 2x and exercise 2x — lose 9 of 30 pounds, mostly healthy eating choices | |
| **Jan** | Maintain visualization 2x weekly, Research coaches <br> Maintain walking and exercise — lose 6 of 30 pounds, 3x weekly flashlight drill <br> Increase Gun Mounts to 3x per week — mostly healthy eating choices | |
| **Dec** | Start visualizations of goals 1x weekly, Walk 2x weekly — lose 3 of 30 lbs. <br> Add exercises from a specific fitness program <br> Use 2x weekly wall chart or flashlight drill <br> 100 gun mounts 2x per week | |
| **Nov** | Enjoying time off — set goals for year <br> Set up off-season and begin dry-firing training <br> Start walking once weekly | |
| **Oct** <br> (The beginning of your season) | Take time off and enjoy time off!!!!!!! <br> Hunting, family, nothing training related | |

## Chapter Summary

Start gnawing on the bit for each shooting competition that lies ahead. For each competition, write down the indicators of how you will perform. Once you do, you'll be headed in the right direction where your technical skills will be strong, your body fit and your mind flexible. And, you'll shoot like nobody is watching in your quest to learn how to win. In the next chapter we'll look at Step 3 of the SportExcel System — GPS. It is your ability to understand that the mistakes and disasters of the game are merely guidance, as they will teach you much, much more than your successes.

Be capable of transforming your goals into outcomes before moving on!

# Step 3

## Guidance is like GPS

*That lousy match really taught me a lesson — not.*

*"Slump? I ain't in no slump -- I just ain't hitting."*

— *Yogi Berra, Star Baseball Player*

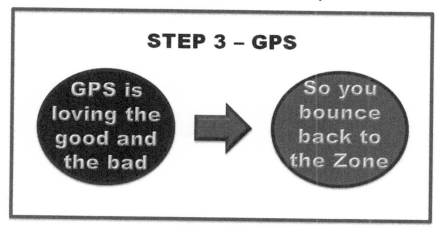

# 9  Your Signal Says Go For It

## *The Zone Signal is fantastic GPS — The secret weapon in your arsenal*

*"Most men stop when they begin to tire. Good men go until they think they are going to collapse. But the very best know the mind tires before the body, and push themselves further and further, beyond all limits. Only when their limits are shattered can the attainable be reached."*

### *— Mark Mysnyk, Star Collegiate Wrestler*

I believe that in sport, there are no winners or losers; only those who actively participate in guiding their mindset in regards to their outcomes, and those who leave it to chance (or to others). When I watch any professional sport, it usually takes me one look at the posture of the coach and athlete during a game to know whether they are either winning or losing. Unfortunately, for most athletes, *The Game* runs their lives instead of them running *The Game*.

*The Game* can be like a two-year-old. It cooperates or throws a tantrum, or more than likely swings back and forth between cooperation and war. Would you let a toddler run your life at the grocery checkout demanding and grabbing for the box of candy bars until he got one? Not likely. But if you allow yourself to get embarrassed by the other shoppers' impatience, you might succumb to the pressure and lose your cool (aka the Zone).

In the same manner many of us let our shooting game get away from us until it runs our lives — embarrassment from squad mates watching us, frustration that the new shotgun fits and performs poorly, anger that the new lessons have produced poorer results than promised. We need to take charge and tame that toddler by staying with the feeling you learned in the previous chapters. Staying in charge of your Zone, and *The Game* — win or lose — will take care of itself and magic can happen. This is Step 3 in the SportExcel System — using GPS-like guidance to manage your Zone.

## Practical Use of the Zone and NO-Zone FEEL

You now have acquired clear signals for being in the Zone — Zone FEEL — and for being in the NO-Zone — NO-Zone FEEL. These signals give you the GPS guidance you need so you can enjoy the Zone in sport and life, as you move toward to your DÉJÀ-VU DVD empowered and inspired outcomes. This GPS is very valuable and the following example will serve to give you an idea of how it works.

Imagine yourself at a traffic light in a busy metropolitan area. The light turns red, yet you force yourself to go through. If you are like most people, you'll feel an internal sensation (a No-Zone FEEL) that says DANGER or STOP or LOOK FOR A COP or AM I INSANE? That is your signal telling you that something is wrong.

Now, imagine yourself back at the traffic light as it turns green — and go through. My sense is that you felt an entirely different sensation, one that said

THIS IS OKAY, where you feel relaxed and at ease. You might check to the left and right before entering the imaginary intersection, but your internal sensation said, "GO." That is your signal telling you that everything is right.

That is how your body acts as your GPS system. Feel the NO-Zone FEEL and you know you have to fix something. Feel the Zone FEEL and trust that everything is a go. Translate that to the station or post, and your body's instant relay of Zone or NO-Zone messages will guide you to the Zone every time and help you stay there. What could be simpler?

## The Need to be Ready

Many athletes and teams have an expectation that one can work their way into the Zone station by station, inning by inning or quarter by quarter. That was my expectation when I played hockey as a young athlete. Sometimes it worked, because in hockey, a team can play dismally for two periods and then they find the Zone and win the game. But when I competed in the martial arts it was a different story. In less than a minute I could be out of the competition after traveling at great expense and time. That is where I learned the importance of being in the Zone from the outset. Waiting to feel good on the podium at the end the match usually ended in disaster. I needed my signal. I needed GPS.

When we travel through a major urban area, we are guided by not one, but many traffic lights. We stop on red, go on green and proceed with extreme caution on amber. Except for rush hour, the system works pretty well. Now imagine if all the traffic lights are cloaked on our side of the intersection and the only way for us to tell if they are red, green or amber is to proceed through the intersection and look in the rearview mirror. It would be very scary and life threatening. Soon every intersection would produce anxiety and fear and we'd be stuck — too scared to move.

And yet that is how many of us compete in shooting competitions. We step into the station or post jittery and nervous — red light — and somehow expect to shoot well. Feeling bad before a round is like anticipating a collision at every intersection. On the other hand, feeling great after running a station or having a perfect round is like looking in the rearview mirror to see that the light *was* green. The purpose of having our Zone FEEL is to guide us to success *before* entering the competitive "intersections" of our sport.

When you feel your Zone FEEL (green light), you know to go for it. When you feel your NO-Zone FEEL (red light) you know to fix whatever the problem is so you get your Zone back — and then proceed. Thus far in this book — to set up this GPS system and to guide you properly — you have been challenged to develop your Zone and NO-Zone sensations to the point where they are as distinct and useful as traffic lights. If you have yet to do so and are reading this book like you would a novel, go back and do your homework. It is the foundation of this system.

When I first learned to play golf, I wanted to impress my partners and anyone else who might be watching. I was nervous, and hoped the ball would go where I wanted it to go. I flailed away at it and, when it travelled to the proper destination, I took my imagined bow to the onlookers. On the other hand, a professional golfer KNOWS where the ball is going to go. He feels his Zone FEEL before he steps up to it. If he hears someone talk or click a camera, he may lose that feeling and step back to shake off the NO-Zone FEEL. Once he feels his Zone FEEL, he knows he is back on track — GPS.

That is the important point to be made here and the only way to play any sport. Being in the Zone dramatically increases the odds that you will be engaging every one of your skills, every component of your physiology and all your positiveness. By doing so, you engage the pleasant feeling, make your competitors disappear, embrace all kinds of weather, accept your equipment and trust your preparedness. You are in the NOW; you are ready to perform; and you have a way of KNOWING you will be successful. The light is green.

## Exercise: Shifting between Zone and NO-Zone FEEL

**1) Stand in front of a mirror and think of a negative memory of a competition that produces the NO-Zone FEEL.** Stay in the memory for about twenty seconds and become aware of your breathing, your posture, and other internal sensations. Look at yourself in the mirror. Notice your facial muscles, your eyes, your jaw and other external features. Not a pretty sight, I imagine.

**2) Now, think of an experience that produces your Zone FEEL.** Get fully into this memory. Notice how your posture starts to shift along with other internal sensations such as breathing. Look in the mirror and notice the changes that are occurring in your physiology. Notice your posture, face and jaw adjust and your eyes become brighter. Notice, perhaps, that you have a wider angle in your field of view versus a narrowly focused one. Feel your Zone FEEL start to blossom as the NO-Zone FEEL fades.

**3) Shift in this manner, from the Zone experience to the NO-Zone experience, three or four times.** Notice how easy it is to shift into the Zone, and, conversely, to fall out of it. You now know how to do it. You now know how it feels — GPS.  Equipped with your own GPS, you will never have an excuse to be out of the Zone again.

What you think about (or what others get you to think about) affects your Zone and predicts how you will shoot.  The mirror tells the story, except you now have a set of internal sensations that allow you to identify and guide yourself into the Zone.  Learn it and use it.

# Chapter Summary

Get used to the guidance of your Zone FEEL and your NO-Zone FEEL.  Get used to shifting away from the NO Zone every time you feel it creeping in.  Perhaps write down what pulls you out — simply out of curiosity.  Become aware of how your body is a natural bio-feedback device, where your Zone FEEL and NO-Zone FEEL are as useful as traffic lights.

As you progress in the SportExcel System, you will need your signals right out there in plain sight (or plain feeling), so that you can stop looking for success in the rearview mirror.  In the next chapter, I will illustrate the type of GPS you can get from self-talk — a very obvious symptom of too much thinking.

# 10 Self-Talk Blues

*Self-talk — positive or negative — will derail your game faster than orange targets on an orange background*

*"I never looked at the consequences of missing a big shot... when you think about the consequences you always think of a negative result."*

**— Michael Jordan, Star Basketball Player**

As a high-performance strategist and trainer I have worked with hundreds of very talented athletes, many of whom who had lost the passion in their sports for any number of reasons. Some are related to past performance, some are related to problems with learning and others are related to athletic self-perception. However, my findings indicate that the number one reason for losing passion is due to a history of having an overbearing, obnoxious or abusive person involved in their athletic life — coach, athlete, parent or competitor. And the number two reason is due to the athlete's continuing to relive the negative effects of this person — long, long after — by way of "self-talk."

# Self-Talk GPS is a Learned Behavior

Self-talk is a substantial part of our GPS guidance system. It is our masterful ability to say nice and un-nice things to ourselves in life generally, and in competitive situations specifically. "Remember to go to the hold point and pick up the target early" is a positive one. It sounds nice, but if your opponent said it you'd be distracted and a bit irritated. And then there is the negative, "You stupid idiot, how could you miss an easy target like that?" the effect of which is self-explanatory.

The difficulty with self-talk is, that although we might be guarded (and sometimes follow) the positive and negative advice we hear from other competitors, when we say the same comments to ourselves they go right into our psyche — unguarded, unquestioned, and unevaluated. Because of this, self-talk is very destructive as it is like having no firewall on your computer to protect against Internet hacking and viruses.

Self-talk tells you that some underlying NO-Zone experience has just surfaced. Listen to shotgunners when the bottom falls out of their game. They give themselves all sorts of advice, most of which is less than flattering. "You've hit this blinking target a million times. How could you be so careless?" It is abusive to both them as well as to the rest of us who have to listen to it.

On the other hand, athletes who are in the Zone have NO self-talk. They might use a few anchor words to do some self-coaching, but they are in the present moment and have no need to listen to positive or negative comments from themselves or others. They just shoot, and it feels good — 'Zone FEEL' kind of good.

# How Self-Talk Gets Started

I had the opportunity to travel to Georgia to work with Coach Mike Simpson and his team of young shotgunners in order to prepare them for the U.S. Junior Olympics. Mike Simpson is one of those coaches whose dedication has had him honored in Georgia State's Assembly as the Volunteer of the Year. He's the kind of coach who forgoes vacations in order to build a shooting facility to keep his world-class shotgunners in training. I admire Coach Mike's work on the trap line. He has a powerful bearing and a voice that is empowering — he uses a kind word with one athlete who might be struggling, and a corrective suggestion to another to keep her in the Zone.

Mike has some amazing stories, and during the course of the weekend he told me about a young athlete he had taken to a national competition a few years ago. At the event, the young shooter had had an extraordinary day and, when they got back to the hotel, where the rest of the athletes were excitedly preparing to call and brag to their parents, this young man told Coach Mike and his teammates that he hoped his dad would *not* call. Ultimately, however, a call from the dad came through.

The young man enthusiastically described his successful day to the dad, but at the end of the call he hung up the phone and fell silent. When Coach Mike asked what happened, the boy reported what his father had said to him: "That's great, but you'll only screw up tomorrow." The next day the father's prediction came true as the young man's game did fall apart. Was the father able to see into the future, or, as we might suspect, did he have a role in the making of it, planting the seeds of the boy's own self-talk?

Another example of the destructive power of self-talk relates to my friend Gordon (not his real name). We played sports together when we were younger and he could be very hard on himself. With nearly every mistake, rather than take it as guidance and fix the problem, he beat himself up and cussed up a storm. On one occasion I had had enough of his outbursts and asked him if he would ever speak to his son like that. He said no and I immediately replied, "Then why do you speak to yourself that way?" He stopped, thought for just a brief moment and then started swearing at me, telling me to mind my own [expletive deleted] business. I had a good laugh (to myself) because my comment stopped Gordon's verbal self-abuse — at least out loud.

Self-talk has to start somewhere, and I believe that we learn to talk to ourselves in the same manner others talk to us. That young athlete's dad and Coach Mike are going to greatly influence this young man's thinking (and self-talk) for the rest of his life. The message of intolerance for mistakes and failure from his dad are going to be the flip side of the message of understanding and empowerment from Coach Mike. Who this young man chooses to model will result in whether he ends up talking to himself like my friend Gordon, his dad or Coach Mike.

## Fixing Self-talk

Why should you fix self-talk? Because it reveals obvious NO-Zone experiences from your past that can be fixed. If you avoid fixing the problem, the self-talk will keep right on doing more damage. Our subconscious minds are very child-like. They take things literally; everything is personal. Self-comments such as "I'm clumsy" or "I'm stupid" or "I'm incompetent" go directly to our subconscious minds and affect us deeply. When you have been talked to in this way as a child, it is very easy for you to continue to abuse yourself, without ever being aware of it. I call it the *self-talk blues*. This is completely unnecessary and, fortunately, easy to change. We just have to catch ourselves doing it — and that can be the hard part.

Spend some time on the shooting range and you'll hear all manner of outbursts from shotgunners. Some curse at themselves. Some complain and whine about their incompetence. Some threaten themselves with bodily injury and death. Some belittle and mock themselves. And how do their bodies react? With hangdog posture, weakness, erratic breathing and worse. Yes worse, because like Gordon, they have heard so much negativity all their lives from others that they often expect that *we* expect them to behave this way after a failure.

To stop this kind of behavior, all you have to do is ask yourself: "Would I talk to another person like this — a child learning to walk, a friend who is learning to shoot, a spouse learning to play the piano?" If you answered no, then fix it. The good news is that you can correct this kind of self-behavior by being a "Coach Mike" type of mentor for yourself when you identify it. Start by shifting to your Zone FEEL and it will probably turn off most of it entirely.

The even better news is that simply by using it as guidance you can get some pretty terrific results fairly quickly. For those of us who are older, it may take more time, but get used to understanding it as GPS and simply apply the tools you will learn in the rest of this book to resolve it. The pay-off is that, aside from our own improved performance, there are tremendous benefits for those around you, whether you are a coach of impressionable young athletes or a parent, squad mate, friend, corporate leader or grandparent.

## Exercise: Curing the Self-Talk Blues

**1) Understand that self-talk is GPS.** In a simple reworking of the GOLDEN RULE, "Treat yourself like you would want others to treat you." It starts with you. Identify your Zone FEEL and get into it at the outset of any competition and maintain it.

**2) When you lose the Zone, listen to how you talk to yourself.** Here are some self-talk examples you might catch yourself saying: "Don't screw it up." "Those targets kill me." "I certainly didn't come to shoot." "Boy did I suck." "The guys in this squad really pull me down."

**3) Shift back to your Zone FEEL if you can and notice how quiet your brain gets.** In the following chapters there will be lots of strategies to help you with this.

One myth in common practice is that we need to displace negative self-talk with positive self-talk or affirmations such as, "I am powerful" or "I am focused" or "I am worthy." The notion is that the more frequently you whisper affirmations of this sort in your head, the sooner they'll become positive, permanent and continuing motivational messages. Quite simply, affirmations require thinking. I suggest, instead, that you use self-talk, once identified, as merely a NO-Zone indicator and fix it.

# Chapter Summary

You now know how you want to be coached, or parented, or talked to. So, do unto yourself as you would have others do unto you. Keep yourself on the pathway to the Zone by being the best coach to yourself that you can be — a Mike Simpson type of coach. Identify your Zone FEEL, identify your

NO-Zone FEEL, and be supportive of yourself as you learn to fix what the self-talk is telling you. In the next chapter, we'll look at a whole range of self-talk type issues that we will now refer to as blocks [to performance].

# 11 Don't Think of Your Big Toe

*The mental blocks — making mole hills into mountains*

*"When anyone tells me I can't do anything...I'm just not listening anymore."*

## — Florence Griffith-Joyner, Star Track Athlete

One summer I walked the golf course with one of my clients and had him practice the skills he had learned with which to stay in the Zone. The golf course was beautiful, the man's game was focused, the weather was exceptional and then it started to turn ugly. Not the weather — me. I started talking non-stop, crinkled a water bottle and told a very a good joke (that he didn't get.) I warned him it was coming, and he listened — to everything.

I was testing his ability to stay in the Zone by setting blocks in the way of his game. Oh yes, he knew his outcome was to stay in the Zone and to play well, but I had my outcome too and that was to teach him a lesson. My outcome was to get him to accept my devious task of undermining his game. And I was having fun planting suggestions for him to plunk his ball in the water hazard, or slice it into the rough, or skip it across the green into the sand.

And I must have been very good at it, because he accepted my outcome very quickly. His first shot did plunk into the water hazard; the second shot lay slightly in the rough; the third was way short of the green; the fourth was a long putt to the hole; and the fifth a two-putt. In summary, I had effectively drawn his attention away from HIS outcome to birdie the hole to my outcome for him of wrecking his game. I set up some very effective blocks to his success.

## The Level of Inattention Triggers GPS

Our level of attention (or inattention) is the product of how powerful our outcomes are. You now know that it is better for us to set deliberate, powerful outcomes rather than let them be set inadvertently by subconscious minds or by others. However, outcomes do get misdirected and we need to identify when that happens, because these types of blocks affect our GPS, even when delivered "out of our awareness" at a subconscious level. Crinkling water bottles, we can challenge; subliminal suggestions from advertisers or hints to miss the target, we can't. People — some devious, some inadvertent — can dredge up and trigger past No-Zone experiences of failure and we are letting them.

## Big Toe Suggestions

In my workshops I demonstrate how distractions work by giving several directives in a row: Don't think of your big toe. Don't listen to the noises outside of the room. Don't notice your breathing. Don't feel your shirt against the skin on your back. With each directive it is clear that the participants are changing their attention according to the directive. Were they attempting to shoot, their minds would be all over the place and I'd be a very successful block to their smoking the target. In the workshop setting, it drives participants crazy

,

and they seem powerless to stop me, at least until they identify what I'm doing — GPS. When they do, that's the time for them to shift gears.

Distracting comments come in all shapes and sizes on the practice or competition range. I'm sure you have heard many of them: "You know that you are only two shots away from a perfect round." "The first station is always the most difficult." "How is the change in your stance coming along?" "Does your arm still hurt?" "Sure is windy." "Man, the clouds make the targets hard to see."

Each statement does a remarkable job of drawing your attention away from hitting the target. Hence, one of the most important rules in any sport is that you get what you think about (or what others want you to think about). So, you must ensure that you control this process in yourself or in the athletes you coach.

## Coach Greevy's Test

Olympic Development Coach and USA 2004 Shooting Coach of the Year, Les Greevy, created an exercise where he deliberately put his shotgunners through a lengthy, rigorous shooting workout and then gave them a practice competition. They were exhausted and shot very poorly. He could have ended the practice and said: "Hey, you guys have had it, let's call it a day." But that would simply have drawn their attention to the block that says: "When I'm tired I shoot poorly." Instead, he gave them five minutes to rest and told them to think about their best competition ever. Just by this subtle change in attention, they did considerably better. He had drawn their attention to their resources of perseverance, skill and determination, precisely what you'll do with the tools you'll learn in the next section, Step 4 of the SportExcel System.

By now you have the prerequisite GPS system in place to identify blocks such as the weather, obnoxious people or fatigue — and you may already be using your Zone and No-Zone FEEL signals to help you. If not, go back to Chapters 2 and 3 and learn the signals. Because when you can identify your Zone slipping away, you will control the process and know instantly that you're going off the rails, have a block to fix or, more specifically, have a negative person distracting you.

And what is even more exciting here is that when you consciously and repeatedly identify and fix blocks, your brain begins to learn how to do it for you automatically. It learns to trigger subconscious correction routines and activate the strategies that follow in the next section. They will help you (and your brain) understand and resolve almost every imaginable block to your game. Your consistency, skills and success depend on it.

# Chapter Summary

Throughout all your practice and competition, you are beginning to learn to identify blocks that pull your attention away from your shooting game. The golfer I mentioned at the outset lost attentiveness when I crinkled a water bottle. Coach Greevy's young shotgunners, on the other hand, stayed attentive even when tired. By identifying and removing your blocks, you too will learn to think "target" instead of "your big toe." So, without further ado, as I've already mentioned the powerful tools offered in Step 4 of the SportExcel System, let's get started fixing your blocks.

Get comfortable with your ability to identify how mistakes and losses affect your Zone FEEL — GPS — before moving on.

# Step 4

## Tools for Success

*Trying to be positive, grounded and present causes us to think.*

**We need tools to help us <u>not</u> think.**

*"What I hear, I forget. What I see, I remember. What I do, I understand."*

**— Confucius, Star Philosopher**

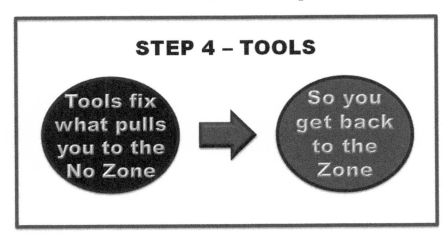

# 12 Block Busters:

# Getting Back on Track

*Learning a new behavior takes 28 days of repetitive behavior — NOT*

*"The difference is almost all mental. The top players just hate to lose. I think that's the difference. A champion hates to lose even more than she loves to win."*

**— Chris Evert, Star Tennis Player**

## Example 1

On my way to present a shooting workshop in Texas, I was listening to a radio call-in show where a woman described her experience with a ghost. She said she was driving uneventfully along the highway when she heard her deceased father yell, "Watch out!" She slammed on the brakes and swerved — and managed to avoid a boulder right in her path. Clearly the woman viewed this as her father's spirit saving her life. However, I view it as an awareness strategy that made full use of her subconscious mind to help her react to adversity.

## Example 2

I was conducting a workshop in Northern Ontario. A participant related a story about how he was piloting his bush plane and the engine quit in mid-flight. Pilots are trained to go through a checklist to restart the aircraft, but what surprised him was that he was doing it from "outside" the aircraft, looking back at himself and giving advice in a very calm, dispassionate voice. He said he matter-of-factly followed the advice and restarted the engine. He felt it was bizarre and had never told anyone to this point. I told him it was simply a subconscious strategy that I teach in advanced workshops to help athletes step back and gain perspective.

## Example 3

A banker friend of mine told me a story of how he successfully shut down a small bank because employees were defrauding the customers of millions of dollars. He described interviewing the manager and the board members, and reading over the accounting books. He told me he had felt uneasy, but there was nothing obvious he could put his finger on. Nonetheless, he called in forensic auditors and they discovered that several million dollars in inappropriate loans had been made. I told him it was one of the best uses of a strategy — albeit subconscious — ever described to me.

## Example 4

A young golfer I was working with had a wildly inconsistent drive off the tee. His father laughed and told me that his son could mimic the drives of 10 or so professional golfers and it was very impressive to watch. I told him that his son's mimicking skill would make him great or be his worst nightmare, as he was using his subconscious ability to copy others.

# Example 5

A shotgunner told me he could slow the target down, make it appear as large as a garbage-can lid and make it turn bright orange at the break point. I told him that this was an incredible strategy that others would pay huge money to have.

# Nothing New Under the Sun

What unifies and connects these examples is the very powerful and effective tools that each of these people used in times of need or crisis. They were subconscious tools — no thinking required. We all have these kinds of tools, whether we are aware of them or not. We use them to create excellence at work or in our sport, maintain our sanity and enhance our ability to connect with others. Sometimes we do not apply them well enough, soon enough, appropriately enough or under duress, but we do apply them.

Think about it. How many times have we heard the following?

"Just breathe between stations."

"Go for a walk and let off some steam."

"Relax."

"Count to 10."

"Step back from this and get some perspective."

"How do you think (insert any name) would handle that shot?"

"Shoot like you do in practice."

"It is just the target and you, nobody else."

Many of these hints or suggestions seem too simple to be useful as tools in our shooting game as we hear them expressed day in and day out. Up until this moment, you might not even have thought of them as tools, and especially not as elite high performance tools. But they are, especially when we can learn simple ways to access them on demand and create a huge impact on our shooting game.

The point I'm making here is that the tools you are about to learn in *Step 4 in the SportExcel System* are simply what every elite athlete you have ever seen already knows how to use. And soon, so will you. They'll be presented in an easy-to-understand format, so that as a novice shooter you can use them consciously (just like you do any new technique in your game) to bust through your mental blocks, and you, the elite shooter, can understand the tools you already use to apply them even better and sooner — just like Paul Giambrone III. You will learn each tool in a step-by-step process and apply them consciously at first. But very soon, with practice, these new tools will operate efficiently at the subconscious level, in the very same way they operate for pros and Olympians. So, follow the instructions, work them diligently and be patient — but not too patient.

# New Ways to Think of Change

With the tools that follow, each and every one of you will learn new ways to break old habits, learn new skills and gain perspective. You will learn what it means to step back and look at problems differently. You will learn how to step into the shoes of your sporting heroes and model any specific skill. You'll learn to step back from a problematic relationship and fix what is bothering you regardless of frustration, anger or irritant. You'll learn to slow down fast targets and make any range feel like it is your favorite. And, with a bit of practice, you'll have all the tools working for you subconsciously, just as the individuals who were mentioned in the opening examples.

# Chapter Summary

You now know how to identify your Zone FEEL and NO-Zone FEEL. You now know how to set and enhance your goals so that they drive you toward success and winning. You know the importance of identifying problems with your game as simply GPS — important evidence that will help you to make corrections and move on to the next level. Now be prepared to learn the tools of Step 4 of the SportExcel System — starting with learning to forget.

# 13 Learning to Forget

*School teaches us to remember the good, the bad and the ugly.*

*Now you're gonna learn to forget.*

*"I never learned anything from a match that I won."*

**— Bobby Jones, Star Golfer**

As a young hockey player I'd often come off the ice after a shift and have one of my teammates comment about a great play or a mistake our line had made. I'd listen and wonder how I had missed it. Was I in the same game? And if it had happened, shouldn't I have remembered it as well? I remember wondering if I was losing it.

This 'forgetting' I had experienced is explained in an article by Dr. Bob Rotella, entitled, "How to Drain 'em Like Jack," in *Golf Digest* (June 2001). The story goes something like this: While speaking with the public, Jack Nicklaus made the claim that he had never three-putted or missed a putt from inside five feet on the last hole of a tournament. A spectator stood up at the end of the talk and informed Mr. Nicklaus that his statement was incorrect and that he had actually seen Jack miss a three-foot putt on the last hole of a Senior PGA event. Jack respectfully denied it, but the man persisted and even offered to send a videotape of the putt. Jack told the man that there was no need to send anything, because he had been there.

When Jack left the meeting, the man persisted and asked why Jack couldn't admit to making a mistake. Rotella, the mediator, asked the man if he played golf. "Yes." Did he have a handicap? "Yes, 16." And, if he missed a putt on the last hole of an important tournament, would he remember it? "Of course I would." Rotella's reply was this: "So let me get this straight. You're a 16-handicap, and Jack Nicklaus is the greatest golfer ever, and you want Jack to think like you?" The man had no answer.

The point of course is that elite athletes only remember what helps them, whereas the average athlete remembers everything. In the early part of Nicklaus' career, forgetting may not have been as easy. He probably felt just as sick about his mistakes as you do. He may even have recycled mistakes over and over in his mind. But he knew what he wanted and he was persistent. It may have taken hours of practice initially but to become great he eventually got it right. And over his career, erasing memories became easier and easier until, ultimately, his memory became subconsciously selective.

## Forgetting Happens Naturally but Why Wait?

Our minds often forget bad experiences over time, simply by the addition and sheer volume of other experiences that are more pleasant. Some memories are resistant to this but, by and large, memories fade or get edged out over time. But why wait for the pleasant to crowd out the unpleasant?

Why wait for the empowering experiences to crowd out the disempowering? Why wait for happy experiences to crowd out the sad? Let's learn to do it now by using our natural ability to mix and jumble memories together in very positive ways.

In the early part of the 20th Century, Russian physiologist Ivan Pavlov performed an experiment where he rang a bell each time he gave dogs their dinner. Before long, the dogs associated the sound of the bell with food, in the same way the typical house pet comes running to the sound of the kibble bag being opened. Simply by ringing the bell, Pavlov could get the dogs salivating for food. The sound of the bell was attached in the dog's memory to food. This is called an anchor — an auditory anchor — because it is directly attached (anchored) to the memory called food — just as a boat is attached to the lake bottom by the real thing, the boat anchor.

As humans, we exhibit the same response to anchors, just as Pavlov's dogs did, and it is an important part of how we learn to avoid that hot stove on the second encounter. Our anchors are many — sight, sound and touch. When a person passes by and waves at us, we feel pleasant (Hey, that person is nice). Even if the person is a stranger, the wave is usually anchored to happy memories and we respond favorably. On the other hand, when a person passes by and gives us a scowl and holds up their middle finger, we have another instantaneous response, probably less than pleasant (Hey, what's his problem?) as that finger gesture is usually attached to negative responses. (I once demonstrated this in a workshop and lost the favor of the participants for a good 30 minutes and have never done it again.) Just like Pavlov's bell produced instant salivation in the dogs, anchors such as these gestures are linked to our human subconscious responses — instant smiling or instant fuming.

# Anchors Away

Anchors attach themselves to all situations. In shooting, great feelings are attached to the light, perfect feel of the shotgun, the crisp, bright image of the target, the warmth of the sun, the flow of our gun mount, the smoothness of our gun swing and the ink-balled target. And bad feelings can become attached to dropped targets, distracting comments, multiple misses, buffeting winds and obnoxious people. The actual response to these anchors can be smiles and adrenalized excitement or curses and tantrums — all of which are triggered automatically — by accidental and purposeful gestures, comments and touches.

But there's good news. We can redirect how we respond to these kinds of anchors. Because of our brain's subconscious ability to be aware of several things at once, we can use the anchoring process to help us forget NO-Zone experiences. We can, for example, take any NO-Zone *moment of disaster* where you remember feeling awful — targets were hard to see, fast, blown by winds, obscured by the background — and mix it with Zone *moments of brilliance* when your shooting felt wonderful — targets seemed slow and huge, there was no thinking and you ink-balled everything. And, just like two different types of metal can make an even stronger alloy when mixed, the memories of your NO-Zone and Zone experiences will be permanently and positively fused.

The following exercise allows you do just this. You'll be creating an anchor to capture a NO-Zone experience, such as Jack Nicklaus' miss from under five feet. And then you'll be creating an anchor to capture a number of powerful Zone experiences, such as the many times Jack won the U.S. Open. And, rather than let the passage of time do the work for you, you'll fuse these two memories together. In the blink of an eye, you'll learn to forget and get back to smoking targets.

## Exercise: FUSING

**1) Take a moment to remember a competition-related, NO-Zone experience that felt terrible.** See it, feel it, hear it. Not pleasant is it? Pinch your LEFT thumb and index finger together. It is the anchor that captures the NO-Zone memory in the very same way Pavlov's bell captured the salivating hunger of the dogs. Release your fingers after a few moments.

**2) Now think of a Zone experience where you were relaxed and comfortable and where the targets seemed to break by themselves.** Relive the memory fully and experience the wonderful Zone FEEL. With your RIGHT hand this time, pinch your thumb and index finger together to capture the Zone memory. This is your Zone Anchor. You now have two opposing anchors, but let's not take chances here. Repeat step two and capture (pinch with your right hand) two more powerful Zone experiences — the stronger the better.

**3) Now you get to have some fun.** Pinch both your left NO-Zone anchor and your right Zone Anchor *at the same time.* There may be initial confusion, but the shift is usually immediate and after a few minutes you'll find it very difficult — if not impossible — to get back to the NO-Zone memory.

## Scarred for Life?  Not.

It is now within your power and skill set to resolve almost any memory that pulls you out of the Zone — weather, backgrounds, obnoxious partners, nervousness, etc. When you drop a target and feel bad, FUSE positive experiences to that NO-Zone. Frustrated with a squad mate? FUSE positive experiences to that NO-Zone. Do you feel your posture slouching and going into the "hang dog" routine? FUSE positive experiences so that you straighten it up. And if it doesn't work the first time, repeat it until it does. The more often you FUSE memories, the quicker and more proficient you will get at forgetting, just like Jack, so the process of forgetting negative experiences becomes an automatic subconscious habit.

# Chapter Summary

As a young athlete I had it right about forgetting the past and staying in the moment. Your ability to fix and forget bad memories, instead of letting them accumulate and cause a downward spiral of misses, puts you on the road to owning your game. When someone says, "Watch out for the wind today" and it reminds you of your worst, windy-day score ever, you'll know how to fuse the memory to great events — so it never returns. In the next chapter, I'll give you further examples of why learning to forget is so important. Before moving on, however, practice the FUSING exercise several more times to ensure you have an understanding of it and can do it "in a pinch.

"

# 14 Love to Miss

*The irony is that the better you feel after dropping a target the fewer targets you'll miss.*

*"Every strike brings me closer to the next home run."*

**— Babe Ruth, Star Baseball Player**

There is sad fact about training in any clay target sport and it is this: The more you practice shooting, the more targets you'll miss. And the more you miss the more it can hurt to miss (even as you might be becoming a better shot.)

Similarly, the more competitions you enter, the more you'll have the opportunity to miss even more targets, at least at the outset. And the more people you meet at competitions, the greater the likelihood that you'll be embarrassed many more times by those missed targets than if you just stayed at home and watched a movie.

# Glass Half Empty

I know I'm looking at clay target shooting via a glass half empty versus one half full, but go to any competition and a huge number of people get very upset by missing targets. So I'm figuring that they must have practiced missing (a lot) to get that annoyed with it or embarrassed by it. So there must be a "glass half empty" group that needs help. Even though they know that missing is part of getting better at the game, accumulated misses are taking a toll on many of them.

So it bears asking the question: Why do we do this to ourselves? Is it the hope of riches and fame? Not for many of us in clay target shooting. So what is it then? Is it the challenge? Maybe, but with the behaviors I've seen across many sports, including golf, a lot of recreational athletes would like it to be a lot simpler. Is it the friendship? That is a given, but many shotgunners might want to read the book: "How to Win Friends and Influence People," by Dale Carnegie. Is it the level of machismo? Perhaps. And even a willingness to be cannon fodder so that others may bask in their glory of victory at your expense.

So besides being an outdoors sport with lots of fresh air and sun, I'm stumped as to why so many would willingly practice missing target after target and:

1) Be nervous at the future prospect of missing them;

2) Get angry at actually missing them;

AND

3) Be distracted by others missing them.

## Enjoying Adversity

I apologize for sounding negative here, but the emotional angst caused by missed targets is serious and there is a better way. I stumbled upon it during my competitive karate career:

*You have to enjoy adversity (love to miss) before you can ever enjoy winning.*

In my case with the martial arts, I had to "enjoy" the pain of getting hurt, whether from my own lack of skill or someone else's over-exuberance.

Allow me to explain. In the sport of point karate, all combatants are supposed to exercise incredible control and techniques (punches and kicks) are supposed to be pulled before full contact. In a wild and furious sparring match, control often gets lost and combatants inadvertently inflict pain upon each other. So, in order to do well at sparring, I had to accept the inevitable pain as I built up my experience. Every bit of pain had to be a motivator — a powerful motivator — to get better and stronger and faster so that I could get more skillful at avoiding pain — or inflict it on others. I had to love every hurt as only then would it lift me higher and higher into the Zone. Once again, this is fabulous in theory.

So I tested a simple mantra: "I love sparring." This little phrase served as something other than an affirmation. It immediately ignited that good feeling of my Zone, something I had rarely experienced at the time, and resulted in a relaxed feeling I'd never felt before in sparring. And once I got used to that feeling, the following weeks and months of training produced huge gains in confidence and fun. It was not pain-free, although it must have helped by producing endorphins to get me through it, as pain usually surfaced on the drive home from the practice or competition.

## Exercise: Love to Miss

In clay target shooting there is pain but it is purely emotional as no one is hitting you with a fist or foot. It is the pain of one dropped target leading to another to another, and this exercise will help you to enjoy that pain:

**1) Remember a rather painful round and watch "this video" in your mind's eye, from start to finish.** You'll be surprised at the kind of detail you'll remember. Notice specifically where you went off track — beginning, middle or end. Pinch your left fingers (FUSING) at that precise moment of dropped target and anchor the NO-Zone feeling — frustration, anger, embarrassment, pain — via the first step of the FUSING strategy you learned in the previous chapter.

**2) Pinch your right fingers as you accumulate three successive Zone experiences where you felt great and powerfully smoked targets.**

**3) Pinch both hand pinches simultaneously.**

**4) Continue to review your "video" and clean up all misses from that round.**

And that is it. You can now replay your memory of your past experience and notice that the "pain" is most likely gone. Vanished. Continue in this manner with any other painful or embarrassing rounds and dropping a target will start to feel good.

The pain of missing must never be carried over to the next shot or a future competition. Learn this approach to missing targets, and you'll likely prevent the second miss from happening, period. And, when you learn to resolve a miss instantly, the death spiral where your game goes out of control will be a thing of the past.

## Chapter Summary

Learn to "love" the dropped target and pre-game or pre-shot fears will evaporate. Once the missed target has absolutely no effect on you, you'll relax and be able to focus on every target, every time, from the first to the last. Make sure after every competition to "re-break" any lost targets. The FUSING exercise works wonderfully here, as you get to copy all your great shots of the past. If, on the other hand, you have had too few great shots, in the next chapter you'll learn how to copy the skills of All-Americans, World Champions and Master Class shooters who have plenty to share.

# 15 Learning New Skills is Child's Play

*As a kid I became my hockey hero, played like him and won like him*

*"The best and fastest way to learn a sport is to watch and imitate a champion."*

**— Jean-Claude Killy, Star Skier**

I have had the opportunity to work with many coaches, athletes, business people, professionals and a mix of professional singers, dancers and musicians from around the world. A common theme, if any, has been that of failure or defeat and the intense emotional content it carries. The FUSING Strategy you just learned works well to resolve this type of disappointment because the athlete already has many experiences of success. It is a very flexible technique that allows them to customize it to individual situations. Their bodies are a vast encyclopedia of knowledge — visual acuity, hold points, strength and power — except when they are faced with something completely new and strange and they then draw a blank.

What if in your shooting career you have only shot American Skeet, where the gun is mounted before you call pull, and then you decide to try

International Skeet, where you must wait for the target to be released before the gun can be mounted? What if all you have ever shot is trap and you are now presented with left to right crossers in the game of sporting clays? What if you are new to the shooting sports altogether and the only experience you have is playing football?

Many times we face situations like these that require new skills. We get frustrated when we try to adapt existing skills — the FUSING strategy — with limited success. As human beings, though, we have an incredible ability to learn new skills by watching others. And as adults, it may simply be a matter of reawakening the learning tools we once took for granted.

## The Blank Slate Gets Filled Up

As kids, we were pretty much a blank slate skill-wise and so we learned quickly. Any frustration was rare or brief. We have no conscious recollection of how we learned; we watched adults and older siblings handle a shotgun and somehow we just knew how to do it too. We watched our heroes, parents and mentors compete and we somehow learned the presence and poise of competing as well. We watched and in the process learned to talk, walk, catch a ball or hit a small orange disk traveling a great speed.

But many of us as adults now find the ease of learning new skills to be more elusive. Perhaps because of pressure, big expectations, self-consciousness or fear, we begin to expect failure and forget how to learn. As a child I played masterful hockey on the pond but when it came to the organized rink — poof — my skill was gone as if in a cloud of smoke. As adults, somehow we need to bypass our fears, doubts and frustrations and get back to an ability to learn and be undeterred by failure. We simply need to see it done and then do it ourselves. Or, do it again and again and again until we succeed like a child bound and determined to walk like his parents.

As a young golfer, I remember going out to the golf course for the first time with my friends and, with rented clubs, shooting par for the course. I look back on that now and muse that it was impossible. But then again, I *didn't know* it was impossible at the time. I was just having fun playing and probably pretending I was Arnold Palmer, my namesake. More importantly, the only place I'd seen anyone golfing was on TV, and they were the best in the world. I realize now that I was doing one heck of a job copying the Arnold Palmers of the world.

Today, what I did no longer surprises me, as I remember displaying similar feats in hockey, badminton and any other sports. I saw an athlete, stepped into his shoes and became him. The way I learned — the way we all learn — is through a process that science has recently discovered where the brain uses what are called mirror neurons (Neuroscientist Vilayanur Ramachandran outlines the fascinating functions of mirror neurons in his talk: **The Neurons that Shaped Civilization**.) It is a natural learning process. As adults, perhaps due to fears, doubts and frustrations, we sometimes block our ability to learn and often consider learning new skills to be the reserve of the young. Fortunately, you can resurrect your natural ability at any age. With an exercise called TALENT MODE you'll be able to learn clay target skills in the same way you learned how to walk, talk and catch a ball, as long as you've seen someone else do it.

# Exercise: TALENT MODE

**1) Think of a shotgunning skill that you would like to improve.** It can involve any situation where you consistently miss a specific target angle, fail to get the stock up to your cheek, shift into an improper shooting stance or lose sight of the target.

**2) Now imagine yourself on a hill overlooking your shooting venue.** Imagine all the delightful sights, feelings and sounds of the beautiful day.

**3) Looking down upon the course, field or range, imagine someone on the right who looks like you, stepping up to call for the target.** That person who looks and sounds like you displays the shaky skill you wish to improve — he or she misses a target angle or fails to shift into proper shooting stance, etc.

**4) Look to your immediate LEFT.** Imagine three elite shotgunners (who have the skills you would like to learn) stepping up beside you. These shotgunners display the kind of excellence you want to have just like Arnold Palmer did for me. You may see them in living color, black and white, or just know they are there, as each of us imagines these visualizations uniquely.

**5) Physically step to your LEFT and imagine stepping into the shoes of the first elite shotgunner.** Notice any sensations in your posture as you do this. Wait a few seconds and then step LEFT into the shoes of the second elite shotgunner. Finally, step LEFT into the shoes of the third elite shotgunner.

**6) After a few seconds, look back out to the course, range or field to your RIGHT and invite the person who looks like you to come back over "inside you."** In this step, you teach that unskillful you what you learned from the elite shotgunners—via their posture and physiology.

**7) Now imagine a future practice or competition where your skill would come into play.** Play it through in your mind and check for the Zone FEEL. If it's there in abundance, go out and test it on the range. If not, redo the exercise until you can feel it. You learned this way as a child and, if it seems too easy, when was learning to walk or talk ever difficult for you then?

# Applying it in Everything You Do

Starting today, I want you to watch shooters at competitive levels higher than you, in person or on YouTube. Absorb what they do without looking for specific technique. After each session, use the TALENT MODE strategy and notice the difference in how you feel. As well, use the TALENT MODE Strategy between stations or posts when you are practicing. In this case, you can simply imagine yourself stepping sideways (so you don't step on any toes.) Be prepared for an accelerated learning curve — especially when you apply it in virtually all areas of your life.

# Chapter Summary

Thus far in the book, you have had the opportunity to learn several definitive skills. You now have the means to acquire the Zone with your Zone FEEL and NO-Zone FEEL signals — Step 1 of the SportExcel System. You have a way to make your dreams of winning come to life with DÉJÀ VU DVD in Step 2. You know that everything that happens to you — the good, the bad and the ugly — can be utilized in terms of GPS, which is Step 3. And now, along with the FUSING, you have TALENT MODE so that you can model both yourself and anyone else in any area of your life — Step 4

This is just the beginning. It is a simple tool kit. Take it out on the shooting range or course and play with it before you move on. And then, in the next chapter, I'll get you walking so powerfully that no competitor will ever bother you again.

# 16 Posture is Everything

*As a kid I slouched, not realizing that posture was both a window to my soul and the means of recovering it*

*"All battles are won before they are fought."*

— **Sun Tzu, Star Chinese General and Military Strategist of Antiquity**

As I was preparing to do a workshop several years ago and speaking with Vicki Ash, one of the best shooting coaches in the country, I pointed out a youth participant who had just walked into the room. I identified his slouched posture and posed the question, "What has happened in his short life for him to hold himself so forlornly?"

I told Vicki that if I did nothing more in the workshop than have this young man walking straight and tall by the end, I would have succeeded in helping him in ways beyond our imaginings, in shooting and otherwise in his life. I remember how he progressed over the course of the workshop, slowly but surely gaining his full height, and how tall he was walking by the end of the workshop. I felt good about his chances in the upcoming national competition — and in life.

## Posture is the Window to Your State of Mind

A person's posture is a clear window to their state of mind, and probably their soul. As you may have discovered thus far, when you change past memories with tools like FUSING and TALENT MODE, the result is a strong and very powerful posture. In this chapter, we will further develop and strengthen your ability to maintain this kind of posture. In doing so, it will not only prevent NO-Zone thoughts from entering your head but will also help you to get rid of them whenever they do.

NO-Zone thoughts thrive when you have a slumped or depressed posture. When you run or walk briskly and your posture straightens, you'll find it very difficult to have a rounded back or slumped shoulders, or the negative thoughts that accompany them. And with that change, depressed moods vanish. So, instead of a traditional therapeutic approach of talking about problems over many hours and days, we need an approach that simply changes our posture and allows that to dictate how we feel.

## Slumped Posture Equals Weakness

Several years ago I had a neighbor who was a promising, young hockey player. I would occasionally notice him walking to school, a forlorn sight, head tilted forward, shoulders rounded, eyes fixed just a few feet in front of him on the sidewalk. Based on his posture, I wondered what negative thoughts were swirling around in his mind: "I hate school." "I didn't do my homework." "I hate my teachers." "My girlfriend is too clingy." My parents are stupid." And add his five-minute walk to the five hours of his school day and you can make some pretty accurate predictions about his performance in hockey that evening. It is going to suffer.

Any person hunched over like this is at a disadvantage, even before the start of a game. The lungs are trapped in tight, constricted compartments and breathing is labored. The spine is compressed, reducing the effectiveness of the nervous system and the signals it needs to send. Muscles are tight, making them slow, inefficient and weak. Now many athletes resolve this kind of posture through the physical exertion and excitement of the game. But by then, in most sports anyway, it produces an incredible waste of opportunity.

Simple shifts in posture affect us dramatically. I demonstrate this in workshops by having a participant hold his forearm above his head, forming a protective karate-type block. I stare directly in his eyes and press down on the arm hard — which usually meets total resistance. Then I have him avoid my gaze and look at the floor. I press down again but with only one of my fingers — and there is usually no resistance. If a simple downward glance like this can wreak this kind of havoc, you can imagine the degree of weakness you create when you slouch. Experience this exercise with a partner; it's eye-opening.

For optimum power and energy, we want to keep our head and eyes straight ahead and we want to keep our posture erect. Simply by doing this, the strength and power we can possess on the shooting range and in everyday life is amazing. I use an exercise called POWER WALK to help resolve and prevent deflated postures, no matter how tough a competition gets.

## Exercise: POWER WALK

1) **Set up a runway A to B (see example below), about fifteen feet long without any obstructions (use a large room, hallway or yard).** Stand in the middle — Point C —and think about a NO-Zone shooting problem, preferably one that causes you to slump.

```
 A          C          B
 _____
```

2) **Walk to Point A on the runway, and "leave" the problem image of you at Point C.** Looking at the Point C image, notice how that "YOU" needs some coaching. Especially notice the posture.

3) **Now, walk powerfully with an imaginary "sky hook" pulling your head erect so that you can feel your spine elongate.** Walking with a comfortable stride, and with some speed, make several passes back and forth from A to B.

4) **After several passes through C, stop and think about your problem.** If it is pretty much gone, you've been successful. If not, continue with several more passes.

POWER WALK can be used to resolve almost any NO-Zone experience from the fear of competition to the embarrassment of a meltdown. It is especially good at getting rid of self-talk — any self-talk. Try the Power Walk exercise (pacing back and forth) before a competition as a simple means of warding off pre-competition nerves. The implications of creating and maintaining the Zone via your posture are seen in everyday professional sports —strong, upright, powerful and intimidating — no matter what the score. As a competitive shotgunner, you need to make it yours.

Starting today, walk powerfully in everything you do, whether practicing or competing, whether at work or at school. It feels good; it keeps self-talk at bay and it makes for an efficient use of energy (in the eyes especially). Lastly, it can be a powerfully intimidating. This is another tool in your toolkit. Practice it and make it an automatic part of your mental game.

## Chapter Summary

So, whether you use POWER WALK as a means to fix NO-Zone memories that weaken you, to prepare for a competition, or to ensure an intimidating air, it can make you feel 10 feet tall and help you to perform accordingly. More interestingly, just as a simple exercise like POWER WALK can make you feel huge, in the next chapter we'll make the targets seem just as big — garbage pail lids come to mind.

# 17 Targets as Big as Garbage Pail Lids!

### *When I'm anxious, the target's a blur.*
### *When I'm on, the target has rings.*

*"A five-goal scorer can tell you the brand name of the pad of every goalie in the league.  I'm seeing the net, he's seeing the pad."*

## — Wayne Gretzky, Star Hockey Player

Most of us will have days when targets are a blur.  Our friends smoke them and we miss them.  In one round the targets are big and bright and in the next they revert to being small and dark.  We search for solutions such as eyewear or gun combs or come up with excuses such as cloud cover, background distractions or brightness.  But, more often than not, you have simply lost your Zone and it can nullify all your training and experience by dulling your senses, particularly your vision.

## Narrow Focus, Fast Targets

When we are frustrated, depressed or highly stressed our vision contracts and becomes much narrower in its focus. Quite literally, our eye muscles freeze and the image is not seen as clearly. (There is a great article on why this might happen called: "*The Reptilian Brain, Dissociation and Seeing from the Core*", by Rosemary Gaddum Gordon.) The contrast in lighting can trick the eye more easily. Items in the foreground and background can take on greater visual significance. Other senses are affected as well. Noises may seem louder and people's voices may seem more obnoxious. Your shotgun may seem heavier and less comfortable. Overall, our brains can sometimes be a lot "noisier" and more scattered and, as a result, targets can seem to be a lot faster and smaller.

Contrast this to days when we feel very good and are in the Zone. All our senses are processing smoothly and efficiently. The targets appear as large as garbage pail lids — big, slow and easy to hit. People and other distractions disappear. The shotgun is a part of our body and target breaks effortlessly with no thinking. It just happens, sometimes so vividly that we get the sense of having an out-of-body experience. The clarity is amazing.

## Training our Brain

If there is any reoccurring theme in this book, it is that our brains have an amazing ability to learn no matter what our age by fine-tuning and developing our senses. In this case, we need to train it to see targets better. The key is the word *train*. We want to train our brains to see only the image we want — that of the clay target — not the background of birds, planes, trees, clouds, mountains, butterflies or fellow shotgunners. We want to train our brains to make seeing and hitting targets so automatic that the targets ink-ball themselves. That's being in the Zone without any stress or fear of failure.

Our brains take in and store information based on the excitement and enjoyment level of an event. For example, if you have been to an enjoyable concert, your memory of the performance will tend to appear large, bright and loud in your mind's eye — memorable. And, if you have been to a terrible concert (or a dull lecture) your memory of the performance is more likely indistinct, small and barely audible — forgettable. Being able to assess the difference in concerts is of little importance, except that our memory works the same way with targets. The unpleasant stress you felt all those days when you struggled to get on top of fast-moving targets is etched in your brain. And the opposite is also true. In your moments of enjoyment, the targets were big and bright and slow.

So, being able to identify the good days and figure out and use "GOOD-DAY" strategies would be very useful. And that is what we'll do via VISTA, an amazing tool that alters the way we perceive targets.

# Exercise: VISTA

VISTA is designed to teach you (and your brain) to shuck off visual distractions and lock onto the target fast. The word "VISTA" means "to see the big picture" and that is exactly what we want a target to be: BIG. This exercise gives you GPS on how your brain typically sees those big target images — garbage pail lid size, perhaps — so you can make perceptual changes to problematic targets to slow them down and sharpen them up.

With No-Zone experiences where we miss targets, we typically perceive them as having weak images that are hard to see, fuzzy and fast, as you can well imagine, or you would never have missed them. Zone experiences, as mentioned, will typically be the exact opposite where we perceive the target as large and slow — a nice target ready for ink-balling. This information gives you the "big picture" of how your brain perceives targets in both your NO-Zone and Zone experiences. And, with VISTA, you get the opportunity to take that information and to make changes.

To do that, you will need to mentally review your mental image of your typical, missed target and compare it to the image of your best, smoked target (the ideal image or template image). And then, you can apply this ideal, template image to all problematic, clay target presentations you encounter in the future.

## 1) The Problematic Target That Got Away

We are going to start with how your brain has stored the information about your hard-to-see target — a NO-Zone target if you will. It is a target that frustrates and embarrasses you when it gets away, usually in a blur, often inexplicably. Imagine this target as you would on the range. Does it appear:

- Focused or unfocused?
- Dark or bright?
- In color or black and white?
- Contained (target in tunnel vision) or peripheral (target in whole scene)?
- Near or far?

There may be similarities with other people, as to how you perceive these targets, but your perception will be distinct to you. As a guide, your GPS for this NO-Zone image might be seeing the target as dark, unfocused, black and white, contained, and distant.

### 2) The Ink-balled Target

This is the type of target, angle or background you love. This is how your brain processes targets that are fun to smash because they vaporize. People stop to watch you when you've got this kind of explosive power. It is your Zone template. Imagine this kind of target as you would see it on the range. Does it appear:

- Focused or unfocused?
- Dark or bright?
- In color or black and white?
- Contained (target in tunnel vision) or peripheral (target in whole scene)?
- Near or far?

Keep in mind that your list will be distinctive to you, and the visual qualities are the ones you will use as your template. As a guide, your GPS for this kind of Zone template might be seeing the target bright, focused, colorful, peripheral and close.

### 3) What's Dark Becomes Bright

Compare the lists you created, as they give you some insight into how your brain has captured and stored information regarding the NO-Zone and Zone memories. Now, in your mind's eye:

a) Place the NO-Zone target image (hard to see target, on a lousy range, etc.) dead center in front of you.

b) Physically reach both your hands straight out — don't be shy — and grab the image. Now stretch the image apart by slowly moving your arms outward to your sides. As you do this, visually add all the qualities of your Zone template. Splash it with some color, force it to move slowly, make it garbage pail sized, brighten it up and zero in on it. Be creative; make it clear.

c) Once you've stretched out your arms as wide as you can, close your hands to the center in front of you. Pull the image apart a second time, but a little faster and with even more of the Zone qualities. Do this process five to ten times over and over, faster and faster.

d) Now think back to the original problematic target. It has probably changed in your perception. If not, redo the exercise and make it as big as a garbage pail lid.

# Test It Out

With VISTA, one can transform virtually every nuisance target into a Zone target, so you can practically predict the end result — a puff of smoke. However, if you can see the target as huge and slow and you're still missing them, it's probably time to adjust your point of impact, replace your shotgun or visit your coach to improve your technique. For beginners who have no memories of shooting excellence, use your experiences in other sports, like tennis, baseball and basketball.

Ask most competitive shotgunners and they'll have targets they like. They may even have preferences for specific target angles and specific lighting conditions. And, on the good days, when all these stars are aligned, they will have the corresponding Zone FEEL where they hit everything. On the bad days, when the stars are misaligned, they will have the NO-Zone FEEL and truly feel the world is against them. VISTA can help you to re-align the stars.

# Chapter Summary

Practice VISTA to transform your ability to see the target by copying and applying your moments of target brilliance — big, slow, sharp and bright. Use it as a regular part of your routine to fix problematic targets or as a warm-up before heading out on the range. To others, it looks like you're shaking off the long drive, but only you will know that you're enhancing the image of the targets you are about to crush. In the next chapter, we'll take your visional acuity a step further and train your eyes to snap to the target acutely and instantly.

# 18  A Lesson from Waldo

*Visual acuity in shooting is either your Achilles' heel or*

*your ace in the hole.*

*"I like going out shooting those tough conditions because typically [other] athletes let it get to them and [they] change up their routine and slip up and miss a few targets."*

## — Vincent Hancock, Star Olympian Skeet Shooter

Perception plays a huge role in all sports, not just clay target sports. In hockey and soccer, for example, it is typical for average caliber players to perceive goaltenders as difficult to beat. And they can be so visually absorbed with the image of the goaltender that the goaltender becomes the target rather than the opening surrounding the goaltender. For these players, goal scoring becomes a two-step process where the athlete sees (1) the goaltender, and then (2) the opening. Elite athletes use a one step process and see *only* the net openings.

It is the same for shotgunners in clay target sports, where the two-step process involves seeing (1) the background — sky, trees, birds, butterflies —

and then (2) the target. When this happens, the usual excuse is that the targets were difficult to see and "nobody" was able to see the targets very well that day. However, even on the most dreadful days, the scorecard usually says otherwise. Some shotgunners score well regardless of the conditions and regardless of the background. And if you ask them why, they might even tell you that it was their lenses. But it is really their ability to take the target in one step, not two.

# What's Good for Wartime Gunners

For shotgunners who complain about the background (or other objects), training can help to eliminate the distractions and get one's eyes to snap to the target. In wartime London, gunners were taught to recognize aircraft shapes instantly. The searchlights might only catch a momentary flash of an aircraft and they had to know instantly if it was one of their own or the enemy. That is exactly what we need to do here, instantly see the target.

A great book that can be used to train your eyes for this purpose is probably one you would never think of. It is a children's book series about a character called Waldo, by Martin Handford. The purpose of this book is to find the Waldo character in a profusion of colorful drawings. But to describe it doesn't do it justice. Take a moment to sneak a copy from your child or grandchild or purchase the book yourself. Most editions of the book are excellent and it is worth acquiring for the following visual acuity drill (and for reading to your children or grandchildren). It is complex and challenging enough to keep you happily engaged for hours. It gives you a rare opportunity to train your visual acuity to very high levels.

# Visual Acuity with a Mental Snapshot

Once you have a ***Where's Waldo?*** book, it is a fairly simple process to find the Waldo character — in seconds. The trick is to (1) stare at the initial example of Waldo on the first page, (2) create a mental snapshot of the image so you get very familiar with it and, (3) effortlessly scan each page of the book to find him. As you engage your subconscious mind in the process, the image of Waldo will eventually "jump" off the page at you in a rather quick and surprising manner.

The images on successive ***Where's Waldo?*** pages get more and more convoluted and confusing, yet it becomes surprisingly possible to find each image of Waldo with increasing speed. Once you have found Waldo on all the pages, you can use the same process to find other images. And, once you have experimented with this for a while, and have found the easy-to-find figures, you can search for the tiniest images, whatever that particular Waldo book offers you.

In the book I had saved after my own children had outgrown it, I experimented with how fast I could find the image of Waldo. It was easy, so I challenged myself to find a tiny toothpick-sized shape that had a dab of red on it — the image of a scroll. Initially I sectioned off the page into a grid pattern and painstakingly explored each section. No luck, but lots of frustration.

I was unsure where to turn next and decided my level of frustration — the symptom of my failing to find the scroll — was merely GPS. So I used VISTA to resolve the frustration, as well as FUSING and TALENT MODE, and then went back to my search. This time I perceived tiny images with bits of white and red, tiny images — probably well-designed decoys, I'm sure — and my frustration grew again — more GPS.

# Getting Closer

Once more I resolved the frustration and, in the ensuing search, out popped many more little decoys interspersed amongst the pictures — quite clearly — and more infuriatingly frustrating. Once more — after which I vowed to quit this colossal waste of time — I once again used the frustration as GPS and the scroll jumped off the page, just like that.

So I can hear you now, "How does finding Waldo or a scroll help me hit the target?" Well, no matter what your level in clay target shooting, finding Waldo amongst the distracting images is the same process whereby your brain finds the target among the background images. If you can learn to eliminate myriad distracting colors in Waldo, you can learn to eliminate background distractions and find the clay target instantly. In the past you may have excused your misses as the result of lack of light, irregular treed background, aircraft or target color. Now, as certainly as you found Waldo in a profusion of background colors, you can now teach your brain to locate the target, especially a bright orange target, in any set of conditions.

The key to creating heightened visual acuity and locking onto the target is to train your brain to subconsciously make the sky, background trees and even the people around you irrelevant. Your "Waldo" skills can be used in the same way wartime gunners picked out enemy aircraft:

1) Engrain the picture of the target in your mind;

2) Use the concept of GPS to stay in the Zone by eliminating frustration or other blocks;

3) Allow your subconscious mind to find the target for you. Instantly.

## Chapter Summary

You have now turned smoking the target into a one-step process by training your brain through the help of a children's book. In the next chapter you'll shift from changing your perspective of the target to changing your perspective of another form of distraction — people. You'll learn to fix intimidating, frustrating and distracting behavior by making it a one-step process as well. Okay, maybe a three-step process, as people can really get under your skin.

# 19 Mind Coach

*If there weren't any people to distract me, I'd shoot*

*really well.*

*"Find your own picture, your own self in anything that goes bad. It's awfully easy to blame your coach or your teammates, but if it's bad, and you're keen on being a leader, you're responsible. If your teammate makes a mistake, you did it. You're accepting leadership. A bad practice, a bad game, it's up to you the athlete leader on your team to assume your responsibility."*

**— Paul "Bear" Bryant, Star Football Coach (as paraphrased by Bob Palmer)**

Imagine how different your current shooting performance would be if your past was only filled with successful experiences. That being unlikely, imagine changing every bad experience you have ever had into a positive one so that you create a sense of having had no bad experiences. No matter what was on the line, no matter what the conditions, you would have only positive memories to draw on. As far back in your memory bank as you cared to look, there would be only the good, the strong and the powerful. This is the SportExcel System. All the exercises learned thus far, from Zone FEEL to VISTA, are all designed to displace and override the NO-Zone blocks that cause you to falter.

# The People Problem

So, now imagine how different your current shooting performance would be if your past was only you and the target — no other people. How much more pleasant the trap-line or station would be with no one attempting to throw you off your game, to distract you with tantrums or to intimidate you with their prowess.

So, you might ask, can I change my perception of them — the good, the bad and the challenging — so they disappear as well? Yes, not exactly the Tony Soprano-style of disappearing, but certainly at the conscious level. We all have people distractions. They can be coaches, wives, husbands, bosses or children/parents; they can be competitors or officials; they can be spectators or the lack of spectators. People do a lot of things to mess us up, both deliberately and inadvertently. However, truth be known, most of the time we have only ourselves to blame. We let them into our lives — and heads — and can just as easily learn to get them out.

A cartoon I often refer to shows a psychiatrist in a chair with his client on the couch. The client complains that his mother always pushes his buttons. The psychiatrist replies that of course she does — because *she installed them.* But for us it doesn't matter who installed them. We own the buttons that get pushed and it is up to us to de-install them, just as we do with obsolete files on our computers.

# Make Opponents Beatable

The "de-install" approach is the same for any number of athletic disciplines. In the sport of hockey, it is often the goalie that intimidates the opposition by appearing huge and imposing. Making goalies "beatable" has huge implications for the morale of a team. In baseball, it is the pitcher to the batter or the batter to the pitcher. How one perceives the other can give an incredible edge in the standoff. In coaching, how the coach perceives the athletes and how the athletes perceive the coach can be motivating or de-motivating. In figure skating, as in other sports, the prospect of performing in front of a crowd can make or break a performance. In the clay target sports, the intimidation factor of both coaches and other athletes can be huge.

# The Psych-out

There is a golf "psych-out" book called: ***How to Win at Golf: Without Actually Playing Well***, by Jon Winokur. I flipped through it in the bookstore and left it on the shelf because it was so different from my leadership approach to winning. I realize now that the book is worth buying for one very good reason — it is an education as to the kind of mind games athletes can face.

A "psych-out" is based upon our amazing ability to make mountains out of molehills, or, in people terms, giants out of normal people. In karate, for example, I was always amazed by one of my instructors who always looked so big and tall, and yet when I stood beside him he might have been a half-inch taller. As he was an amazing fighter, and a number of belt levels higher than I was, I considered myself fortunate not to have to fight him in a competition.

Many athletes have the necessary technical skills, but at the subconscious level envision themselves as less significant or even insignificant when comparing themselves to other athletes and, as a result, are easily intimidated and defeated by presence rather than skill. These athletes need to step back and get a new perspective on the situation. How many times have coaches (or parents or teachers) suggested that we cool down and count to ten, or step back and open our eyes to how our opponent is taunting, teasing or otherwise irritating us? How can coaches see this but not us? Well, there *is* no good reason and with a strategy called MIND COACH we'll become our own self-coach.

## Exercise: MIND COACH

**1) Think of a competitor (we'll call him John) who negatively affects your game.**

**2) Imagine you're in a theatre.** The stage lights come up on one side of the stage and he appears. Pick one word that describes his behavior — no swear words please. In this example, we'll call him "intimidating."

**3) Now notice stage lights come up on the other side of the stage, and you are looking at YOU.** Pick a word that describes YOU on stage in the context of shooting against John. How about "nervous?"

**4) Now, ask yourself the question, "Who is leading whom?"** Is John leading YOU or vice versa? I believe you'll find that indeed it is John who is leading you, whether he realizes it or not.

**5) To get on the leaderboard, you'll have to take leadership.** So, in your mind's eye, go down to the YOU on stage. Put that YOU in the Zone, make him ten feet tall. Make him absolutely invincible.

**6) And lastly, step into the shoes of that YOU on stage and feel that new strength, power and confidence.** Take one more look at John and you'll notice that he too may have changed — diminished perhaps?  Now go test out your newfound leadership skill — and notice how John reacts to it.

# Don't Trust Anyone

A while ago I watched as that same karate instructor I mentioned earlier lost in an early round to an opponent he should have beaten easily.  A few months later I cornered him at a Christmas party and asked him what had happened.  He told me that he too was puzzled.  I asked him if he wanted to find out.  He gave me a puzzled look and said yes.  So I then took him through the MIND COACH exercise to give him some insight and had him go back to the memory of the competition.  He immediately started to laugh. What did you notice? I asked.  He didn't beat me in the ring, he said.  He beat me in the warm up.  I never talk to anyone before a match and he came up to me and mocked me, in what at the time seemed a humorous vein.  He laughed again and then indicated to me that he would never let that happen again.

# The SportExcel 30-Minute Rule

In the sports world, as I inferred in previous chapters, it is common for players and even coaches to subtly give advice, create doubt or plant suggestions before a competition.  MIND COACH is essential here, as this has prevented many of my athletes from falling into the same trap.  However, one tip is to stay away from everyone a good 30 or more minutes before your competition to prevent people from getting inside your head — period — because, believe me, some are very good at it. I call it "The SportExcel 30-Minute Rule. Use the time to get into your Zone, rehearse your competition with DÉJÀ VU DVD and take on all comers with MIND COACH. And take my advice, "Don't trust anyone!"

# Chapter Summary

The applications for MIND COACH are endless and can be applied to all areas of your life — from taking leadership to building relationships to dealing with bullies in school. Practice it just like the other tools and you will find yourself minimizing the negative effect that opponents, audiences, parents and coaches have on you. Become sensitized to the fact that athletes and their coaches will attempt to psych you out, whether intentionally or unintentionally. Refuse to play that kind of game. Instead, call them on it if necessary or simply use MIND COACH to fix it and move on. In the next two chapters, we learn how coaches and parents can use the same exercise for building leadership skills and developing coaching/parenting strategies.

# 20 The Coach as Emotional Ballast

*That kid will never win a karate competition — Oops,*

*did Sensei Bob just say that?*

*"A good coach will make his players see what they can be rather than what they*

*are."*

— *Ara Parseghian, Star Football Coach*

As a high performance trainer, I work with shotgunners who shoot near-perfect scores in practice and then falter in competition; I work with baseball players who falter when facing critical situations; and I work with football players who are extremely quick thinking in practice but make mental errors under pressure. In most sports it is called choking, a phenomenon that every athlete has experienced at least once. As frustrating as it is, it is easy to fix, especially in an athlete's early years. This is because it is likely a coach has caused it in the first place.

Now, if you are a coach, please don't be embarrassed if this comment strikes a chord, and certainly take your fingers off the keyboard regarding "a letter to the author" complaining to me if it angers you. I say this because it is the caring side of coaches that gets them in trouble. Most coaches are very passionately concerned for their athletes' wellbeing, and they can cause their athletes to falter precisely because of it.

## That Sinking Feeling

As a coach, when one of my karate students made a mistake and lost a match, I would generally feel their angst through a sinking feeling in *my* stomach. This very real connection — this direct pathway between coach and athlete — is what makes us caring and compassionate individuals. But at the same time, when we feel an athlete's disappointment it can also make us less than effective coaches.

Why? They see and especially feel our concern but have no way of telling the difference between our disappointment *for* them, and perceived disappointment *in* them.

## Too Much Empathy

As coaches we need that empathy for our athletes, but we also need to know how and when to turn it off. Rather than follow our athletes into whatever state they get into, we need to exert leadership. I call this role the emotional coach, where at any time, no matter what troubling thoughts an athlete is thinking, he or she can always turn to the coach and feel the coach's Zone. Yes, the Zone. Watch most high school basketball or football games and you'll know why they expect the opposite. And that is so wrong. It can also be disastrous.

To mirror back to athletes their worst fears of failure, frustration and disappointment is to confirm that they should be disappointed. They have failed, so they must accept that they are failures. Worse yet, it is almost as if we are trying to ingrain and reinforce that they acted stupidly so each time they pick up a shotgun they will remember to (never) mess up again. It is a less than favorable approach, as it actually encourages thinking about past mistakes.

As coaches, we need to stay in the Zone and avoid reinforcing their expectations. When they make a mistake, turn to us to have it confirmed and instead get a powerful Zone reaction, imagine the bewilderment. And that bewilderment — brought about by the athlete's seeing and mirroring *our* Zone — allows him or her to recover spectacularly fast and get right back into the game. It is very cool to watch. Two teams can make the same number of mistakes and it will be the team that recovers the quickest from mistakes that will win. This kind of coaching approach encourages that kind of fast recovery.

To stay in the Zone as a coach is to believe that athletes have to:

- Develop the resources that are required to thrive on pressure;
- Experience losing in order to build resilience;
- Experience intimidation in order to counter it;
- Deal effectively with losing in order to become a champion;
- Observe the coach as a role model of how to handle adversity, develop a work ethic and create a powerful Zone.

That said, here is my Number One rule in coaching:

## If I stay in the Zone, my athletes will.

As coaches we have to draw on our own personal history of skills and strategies to model the kinds of behaviors we expect of athletes. Remember — and we often forget this — competition is wholly new to young athletes and whatever impression it makes on them can last their entire lives. The coaches who understand this rule are often amazed by the effectiveness of doing just this and little more on the mental side of training.

## Exercise revisited: MIND COACH

For a coach, being your athletes' emotional ballast can be a lot of fun. For many coaches, it is both a physical and a philosophical shift — but we have to have easy and practical ways to implement the change. In the previous chapter I introduced you to MIND COACH. Here it is in a coach's version:

**1) Think of an athlete (we'll call him John Jr.) who struggles at competitions;**

**2) Imagine you're in a theatre where the stage lights come up and reveal John Jr.** Pick a word that describes his behavior. For this example, we'll call him scared;

**3) Now notice that a spotlight has come up on the other side of the stage and there is an image of you, the coach.** Pick a word that describes the YOU on stage. We'll label him "concerned;"

**4) Now, ask the question, "Who is leading whom?"** I think you'll find John Jr. is in full control of your emotions, inadvertently, I'm sure. But since you are the coach and the leader, you might want to take back leadership. So in your mind's eye, go down to the YOU on stage. Put that YOU in the Zone — 10 feet tall and inspiringly powerful;

**5) And lastly, step into the shoes of that YOU and feel that new strength, power and confidence.** Then take a peek at John Jr. He could possibly be looking entirely ready to take on all comers, now. Of course, now you'll want to test out if this is really as effective a coaching tool as it sounds.

Over my 20 years of teaching karate, I frequently used MIND COACH to tailor my coaching style. One particular student I'll call Mary was a case in point. She typically came to class in a disheveled uniform, stringy hair and an attitude that I took to mean, "Just you try to teach me anything." Even in her first class, I thought, "She'll never survive." And following the typical "oops, did I say that?" I plugged her into MIND COACH and continued teaching. I certainly had no idea of how I was going to make her karate career a success, but, after doing the exercise only once, I could feel the passion that I, as coach, would require.

Mary's transformation was slow and steady after that. She formed friendships with other classmates and even started to attend tournaments. Of course, the other students consistently came back with trophies, and Mary always stood out in those pictures, the one without one. She just lacked something I couldn't put my finger on and again I caught myself saying: *That kid will never win a karate competition. Oops.* Once again MIND COACH came to the rescue.

And then it happened. Mary was in the finals of point sparring at the national championship. I could taste the medal — a first or second guaranteed — and the only way Mary could lose it was to hit her opponent in the face and get disqualified... which she did. My shoulders sagged and my heart when out to her, but I quickly recovered my Zone so we could make the best of it. But when the officials presented the medals for kata forms first, Mary received the bronze—unexpectedly she had her first medal. She beamed; I beamed. And believe me, the celebration that ensued produced more than a few tears and still stirs up emotions when I retell the story today.

More often than not, helping athletes such as Mary get the most out of their performance is simply a matter of knowing that you can. It is your ability to step back via MIND COACH and create a new perspective. You get to see how your leadership behaviors — both good and bad — affect the behaviors of your athletes. And it gives you a second, third and perhaps infinite chance to get it right. Give it a shot and see how much you can increase your enjoyment in the game, as well as that of your athletes.

## Chapter Summary

Mind Coach ensures that your athletes stay in the Zone no matter what mistakes they make. The only meaning for "choke" they know is as a means to affect their shotgun's shot pattern. MIND COACH is the rehearsal that will keep you and your athlete on target. You are helping them perform — and YOU will need to put on the best performance of THEIR life. And, if you are a parent (or even a grandparent, boss, etc.) who thinks the same kind of approach could work for you, the next chapter will include you in the game too.

# 21 The Parents: A Coach's Best Ally

*Take your ear buds out and talk to me about the competition — I drove you, didn't I?*

*"Leadership [parenthood] is a matter of having people [your kids] look at you and gain confidence, seeing how you react. If you're in control, they're in control."*

**— Tom Landry, Star Football Coach (as paraphrased by Bob Palmer)**

In the previous chapter I wrote on the topic of coaches being the ballast for their athletes and the incredible results they could get from this simple philosophical shift. I purposefully neglected to describe one of the key players in the process — parents. I'm very supportive of parents of young athletes because I was one, and I know what they go through. They spend more time with the athlete than the coach and yet often feel undervalued by both the coach and the athlete. They also get blamed for the many behavioral sins of their child.

The main way parents find to get around this is to stay home. Another is to watch the event covertly from behind a tree. This chapter is aimed at parents who wish to overcome this stigma and actually be a benefit to both the coach and their child.

# Coach Greevy's Shooting Camp

When I first started working with Coach Les Greevy's Olympic Development Team in Pennsylvania, the parents of his athletes were having challenges with their children. The athlete would drop a target and feel bad and the parent would feel bad as well. The child would further collapse and cry and the parent would have tears welling up in their eyes as well. This emotional loop between child and parent would spiral downward out of control with mom (or dad) in the stands in an agonized, emotional dance with the child on the field. And they were only doing what parents do well, empathizing with their child.

So, here is parenting rule number one:

## If I stay in the Zone, my child will.

Sound similar to the coach's rule in Chapter 20?

To help resolve the dynamic between parent and child, Coach Greevy borrowed time from our athlete workshop to address the issue with the parents. I treated them like coaches and introduced the golden rule.

# Parents Are NOT Spectators

"You mean we can't just be spectators?" was one parent's response. I told them that they *could* be spectators and follow the emotional ebb and flow of their children's performance, or they could be emotional coaches and remain in the Zone (leadership) for all the ups and downs of any competitive activity. No matter where you sit, I added, your child will locate you. And when they do, your Zone can influence them in exciting and powerful ways

To emphasize this point, I described a skeet shooter who mostly traveled to competitions with his family. One time he traveled with his dad, another time with an aunt or an uncle. Occasionally he traveled with his coach. Over the course of several tournaments a pattern developed: When he traveled with his family he shot horribly, at least in the initial rounds of competition, and when he traveled with his coach, he shot well and even won a national collegiate competition.

I told the parents that the trip with family was superficially about the shooting, and mostly about sightseeing and expectations, squabbles and grandma's troubles and the cost of the sport and the price of gas and the business call on the cell phone. On the other hand, the trip with his coach was all about shooting, stories of past competitions, stories about hunting, stories about all manner of things related to shooting. In this light, the latter experience with the coach wires the athlete's mental circuitry for success.

## Parents Are Emotional Coaches

At this point I could tell that the parents were concerned. How could they compete with any coach? I told them to not even try. They did not have the technical skills or experiences that relate to becoming a shotgun coach. But they did have the maturity and life experiences that relate to becoming an Emotional Coach.

I told them that I was an Emotional Coach with my daughter the equestrian. Now, I know very little about the sport except that horses are big and unpredictable. But I would watch her ride and be a little disappointed by her slowness to pick up on some of the finer points. After all her years of lessons, she was still being asked by the coach to adjust her cadence.

I told the parents that during one of these lessons, it occurred to me to practice a little of the medicine I was preaching. I left the stable, went to my car and took myself through the MIND COACH exercise. What I visualized shocked me. I could only see my daughter spinning in circles on the horse. Perhaps I was scared for her. Good guess. With that insight, I (Emotional Coach Dad) quickly fixed the spinning, at least in my mind, got in the Zone and returned to watch my daughter. And to my amazement, the rest of the training session was spectacular. No more issues with cadence. Wow. My fear clearly had had a huge impact her. The parents smiled knowingly.

## Exercise revisited: MIND COACH for parents

**1) Think of your child (we'll call him J.J.) who keeps his ear buds in and doesn't want to talk before, during or after competitions.**

**2) Imagine you're in a theatre where the stage lights come up and reveal J.J.** Pick a word that describes his behavior. For this example, we'll call him "inconsiderate."

**3) Now notice that a spotlight has come up on the other side of the stage and there is an image of you.** Pick a word that describes the YOU on stage. We'll call him/her "angry."

**4) Now, ask the question, "Who is leading whom?"** I think you'll find J.J. is in full control of your emotions, inadvertently, I'm sure. But since you are the parent and the leader (and have years of emotional self-control), you might want to take back leadership. So, in your mind's eye, go down to the YOU on stage. Put that YOU in the Zone — 10 feet tall and inspiring.

**5) And lastly, step into the shoes of that YOU and feel that new strength, power and confidence.** Then take a peek at J.J. He could possibly be looking like he wants to talk about the competition. Of course, now you'll want to test out if this is really as effective a parenting tool as it sounds.

Communicating with your child is a big challenge, but the parents who have adopted this perspective rave about the positive effect it has had on their family. As parents, you naturally spend an inordinate amount of time being chauffeurs to your kids, so you might as well use this time with them in mind instead of conducting business on the cell phone or mindlessly listening to the radio. The Zone is contagious. Twenty minutes seated beside you with your full attention will be energizing for your child. An hour will be dazzling. One hockey parent has been using this approach for several years to get his son in the Zone before his skates hit the ice. And last I heard the kid has just signed his first pro contract.

# Chapter Summary

With MIND COACH, you have a powerful leadership tool to get your child ready for practices and competitions — Zone ready. When you hand over your young shotgunner — in the Zone—to his or her coach, the coach will love you for it. And, by using MIND COACH to create a strong Emotional Ballast for all your kids' activities, you will help them to build confidence, self-esteem and skill for life. They might even want to talk to you. One of the ingredients you'll be evoking to get them ready is adrenaline. And in the next chapter, we'll all learn how to manage it for a practice or competitive event — child, adult, coach and competitor.

# 22 Drug of Choice: Adrenaline

*Ramp yourself up and manage your adrenaline all day,*

*every day.*

*"It is the greatest shot of adrenaline to be doing what you have wanted to do so badly. You almost feel like you could fly without the plane."*

## — Charles Lindbergh, Star Aviator

While working with several female figure skaters, I ran up against a wholly unexpected problem: They are too demure and quiet. They spent long uninterrupted hours on the ice practicing and the only thing they had to fight was their own self-confidence. As a result, they were like emotional pinballs, knocked hither and thither from emotional crisis to emotional crisis, mental block to mental block, distraction to distraction, coach's tantrum to parent's tantrum. They needed an adrenaline boost to give them some oomph, so I pulled out one of my punching bags and had them kick it hard, very hard. Only once did I have to say that they kicked like girls before they nearly bowled me over. Figure skaters have very powerful legs! And once they got a taste of that power, and the adrenaline that goes with it, their eyes sparkled and they wanted more.

# Contact Sports Generate Continuous Adrenaline — Not

Compare figure skating to football, where athletes have extensive body contact and the pure adrenaline rush of explosive power. Speak to these players and they'll mention their addiction to the adrenaline rush of hitting everything in sight. Add to this their coaches, who get very excited and exuberant and even encourage aggressiveness as a means to raise adrenaline levels. They are quite a different lot, these nervous, adrenaline-sated football players. But, sad to say, it is often a crapshoot as to whether or not football players are any more "adrenalized" than figure skaters. The same is true in most sports.

Generally football players know to start the game pumped and ready for action. They scream at each other, hit each other on the pads and have mock one-on-one battles. But, after the game begins, that adrenalized edge is slowly diminished or lost entirely as the adrenaline seeps away. And once that happens, it is very hard to get it back with any degree of certainty.

# Pinball Emotions – the Ebb and Flow of the Game

Talk to any athlete or coach and they often speak of *momentum* rather than adrenaline. They speak of tennis matches where one athlete will be down a few sets and slowly the momentum will shift in favor of the other. They speak of golfers who suddenly find the Zone midway in a round and move to an effortless swing. They speak of Olympic-level skeet shooters who allow their routines to run effortlessly and mindlessly. We call this momentum but in pure chemical terms it is a stable supply of adrenaline.

These comfortable "adrenalized" states often occur in the middle of competitions when, in my experience, the bags may already be packed for home. If you are not in the Zone at the outset of any match, expect a struggle. It is at best wishful and misguided thinking to expect momentum to build over the duration of the game. Think of it as a drag race. Both cars build momentum over the course of a quarter mile but the one with the best start and the fastest acceleration wins. Imagine the advantage one of the drivers would have if he hit the start line at full speed. Now, imagine applying that principle to adrenaline in a clay target competition.

# Creating My Own Adrenaline Fix

How much adrenaline does one need to ensure momentum? How much will entrench us in the Zone so that nothing can pull us out? How much is too much, too soon? I was able to answer these questions via karate and I did it in practice sessions by trial and error. First I fled to an isolated region of my house — my basement — when nobody else was home and put on a display more befitting a crazy man. I jumped and screamed and shadow boxed imaginary competitors. I screamed karate yells that even unnerved me — bloodcurdling perhaps.

Initially, I felt a bit wonky (not to mention self-conscious lest the basement's walls be too thin and unable to muffle my yells). I got rubbery legs and glassy, teary eyes. But then I got used to the adrenaline and it felt good — very good. After several sessions of this in the basement, along with testing it in practice, I got to the point where I knew precisely how much adrenaline I needed and when. It was a very interesting experiment. The more I pushed myself to higher levels of adrenaline, the easier it was to trigger and control.

Next, on the day of competition, I planned when I would bring on this pre-programmed hyper-adrenaline (not over-adrenaline) state of being. And, it was very exciting, because after I learned to trigger it on demand, I rarely lost a match. I was that drag racer who was going at full bore at the start line and my opponents never even saw the blur that would pass (beat) them before they knew it.

## Exercise: The A-Button (the Adrenaline Button)

This exercise will help you to pre-program yourself to "adrenalize" appropriately before any practice or competition. All it takes is pushing the right button — your Adrenaline Button.

**1) Pick a spot on your body to be your A-Button.** (It is an anchor, very much like the anchors you used in Chapter 13.) Choose a spot that is easy for you to touch but is safe from being accidentally triggered, for, as one of my shotgunners discovered by accidentally triggering it at bedtime, you may be in for some sleepless nights. Locations on your body that you might use are:

- The fleshy part of the hand between the thumb and the index finger
- The base of the wrist
- The crook of the elbow
- The tip of the nose
- The earlobe

**2) Now, remember experiences where you had plenty of adrenaline.** A professional surfer I'm working with uses bungee jumping as one of his. Or, you can aggressively shadow box like I did. Or you can remember a clay target or other sport-related experience. In any case, feel your adrenaline and anchor it to your A-Button.

**3) Over the next few days, repeat the exercise several times.** You will know when your A-Button is working properly as you will get a surge of adrenaline whenever you touch it. Keep adding new Zone experiences to it to refresh it, especially after competitions where you might have relied on it a lot.

As far as evoking your adrenaline for competitions, the following simple graph shows the amount of Adrenaline (%) on one axis, and the time (time of the competitive day) on the other. When you wake up you need to be at X % adrenaline. When you drive to the venue you need to be at Y%. When you

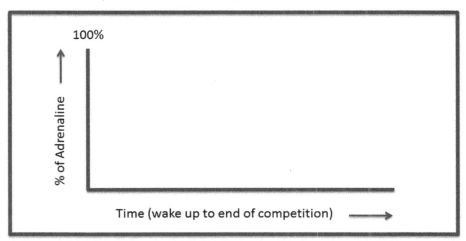

step onto the field, range or course, you need to be at Z %. With the first target, you shift fully to 100 per cent fueled and ready to go. And, of course, your A-Button is always at your fingertips to give yourself a shot when you need it.

Like any skill, managing your adrenaline level will take some time and practice. With wise management, your body will learn exactly how much you need and when you need it. Eventually you will be able to quickly move into and out of it — at will. But be careful: A young hockey player I worked with made the mistake of firing his adrenaline at the start of the school day and then had none left by the time of his game that evening. Manage your adrenaline output wisely — put it to use when it will be most effective.

## Chapter Summary

Just as I've had figure skaters slugging away on punching bags and myself shadowboxing in my basement, shotgunners need to create a powerful and accessible supply of adrenaline if they want to win. As well, just as it has to be carefully crafted, it also has to be monitored and adjusted — a process we'll tackle in the next chapter.

# 23 Never Stop Moving

## *Adrenaline — Use it or lose it*

*"Ninety percent of my game is mental. It's my concentration that has gotten me this far. I won't even call a friend on the day of a match. I'm scared of disrupting my concentration. I don't allow any competition with tennis."*

## — Chris Evert, Star Tennis Player

I remember watching the video of a karate tournament in which I had competed. Before the start of the match, the head judge was giving instructions to the black belt combatants, all of whom were standing stock still, except one. He stood out very clearly, a bit silly looking, shifting from foot to foot like a single tree swaying in a perfectly still forest. I looked closely at the person and realized it was ME!

## Intuitive Shifting

Now, however, I understand that what I was doing was anything but silly, albeit intuitive. I certainly remember feeling good, and was surely in the Zone, moving to keep my body loose, moving to maintain the adrenaline that

I had built up while warming up.  I also understand now that my adrenalized swaying was blocking everything else out — my fellow competitors, the judges, the noisy spectators, internal self-talk.  Had I stood still, I likely would have felt uncomfortable (as I would have felt my adrenaline seeping away).  As for looking silly, that would have been the farthest thing from my mind as that would have required caring about what other people thought of me — which is no way to compete.

In addition to keeping me in the Zone and keeping thoughts out, I soon realized that the swaying had other benefits.  When I was training a cross-country ski team for national and international competitions, the coach, a former Olympian, reminded his athletes that awareness of technique in competition is a distraction, as by pushing technique thoughts out of your head, you are trusting that your body and mind will deliver what you need at the time you need it.  Nice confirmation.

The shifting stops you from thinking, forcing you to trust the skills you've been practicing — the prerequisite to performing subconsciously. Fueled with sufficient adrenaline and feeling your Zone FEEL, you keep your brain running optimally with no need to think. This is similar to your skills driving a car where, with experience, you can adjust the radio, eat a burger and chat with fellow passengers, all at the same time — with no thoughts of your foot pressure on the gas pedal, grip tension in your hand on the steering wheel or the road vibrations on your backside.  Your driving skills work subconsciously.  Driving is a FEEL game.  Shooting needs to be as well — skills, strength, visual acuity, agility and smoothness, etc.

The following exercise will help you to develop your 'feel' game and utilize a constant swaying motion to do so.  It will keep you trusting your technique, experience and preparedness — without having to think.  You will simply run on automatic, fueled by adrenaline.

## Exercise: POWER SHIFT

**1) Stand upright and imagine that a person is standing beside you, only slightly off your line of center.** That person looks like you, when you are in the Zone.

**2) Shift from foot to foot into and through this image, back and forth, repeatedly, like an inverted pendulum.** Each time you pass through the image, notice that you can feel your Zone FEEL.

**3) Continue to sway in this manner and allow the adrenaline to super-charge your Zone.** It will displace all other thoughts and you'll notice that there is no thinking.

Our competitions allow us ample opportunity to stand still and become sitting ducks for comments, visual distractions and sounds. POWER SHIFT ensures that you keep moving. It was what I was doing at the karate tournament, what many professional athletes do during the singing of the national anthem in preparation for the game, and it is what you'll need to do in the minutes leading up to your competition and between posts, stations and rounds. It may look odd on camera and it may irritate your opponents but no one will enter your headspace and you will never be wanting for adrenaline. If you are a competitor who knows your outcome, feels your Zone and trusts in your technique, it helps you to stay in the Zone all the time — and on the leaderboard.

# Chapter Summary

By swaying, you displace thoughts about score, weather, your competition, your work, etc. It keeps the Zone simple and powerful and adrenalized.  It is the last of the tools in Step 4 of the SportExcel System. Now, just like you need to trust that your shooting skills will work for you without thinking, you also want to trust that the skills you are learning in this book are working for you — without having to think about them either.  Our subconscious minds really are very capable of doing this — with little or no conscious thinking.  In the next section, Step 5 of the SportExcel System, we'll find out how.

Put one tool at the top of each day on your calendar or smart phone and practice it that day until you understand and can use it effortlessly.  Repeat as needed.

# Step 5

## The System

*The beauty of setting up a system is that it will work for you and make your life a lot easier, even when you are sleeping.*

*"Success isn't something that just happens - success is learned, success is practiced and then it is shared."*

— *Sparky Anderson, Star Baseball Coach*

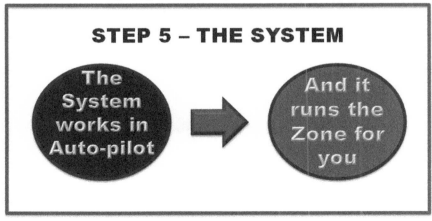

# 24 Building Trust: On Autopilot

*Keep the Zone running 24/7*

*"Before I'd get in the ring, I'd have already won or lost it on the road. The real part is won or lost somewhere far away from witnesses - behind the lines, in the gym and out there on the road, long before I dance under those lights."*

**— Muhammad Ali, Star "Float like a butterfly, sting like a bee" Boxer**

Just as many of you anticipate a season of clay target shooting, I look forward to a summer of recreational golf. Ah, warm summer days, great enduring friendships, singing birds, gem-green landscapes. In this idyllic setting, one can almost hear gentle symphonic music in the background. Why, it is so beautiful it begs the old expression, "A bad day on the golf course is better than a good day in the office."

If you knew my dark sense of humor, you would be waiting for someone to jar the CD player to start the beautiful music st-st-st-stuttering.

Golf, shooting or any other sport, whether recreational or competitive, is rarely like that. In the brief moments when you are hearing yourself say that you love the sport, there is another person who insists on thwacking the CD player. In very pleasant, under-the-radar tones during normal conversation, he or she will say: "Hey, you're shooting well, what are you doing different?" Or, "That new gun seems to be working great." Or, "Those targets sure are unpredictable with that wind." Or, "That machine's not throwing good targets, is it?"

As I've previously stated in this book, to be in the Zone you must be shooting in a kind of trance at the subconscious level. The probable intent of a partner's statements is to break the trance and bring you back to the conscious realm. The partner might as well be saying, "Hey, you're not thinking of anything but shooting (i.e., you're beating us) and we need to get you to think about something else."

## Unconscious Competence

A skillful Zone is often referred to as Unconscious Competence — you don't have to think about what you're doing anymore, you're just good at it subconsciously. This requires incredible TRUST in your abilities, and, when you are in this state, shooting is easy. There is no self-talk and especially no easy explanation of what is happening; it just happens without thinking. (Sometimes it even seems that we are watching ourselves shoot.)

I learned about subconscious competence through karate. At the time, I was good at sparring but reluctant to compete because I second-guessed myself and listened to all manner of self-talk. "Jim has long legs, so go in tight; Bill is fast, so give him some distance; Richard is tricky, so watch his fakes." I became more concerned about what they could do to me rather than what I had to do to them, and I forgot to fight. I had no trust in my ability to protect myself — I was scared.

In hockey it was different. I not only trusted that my legs would skate for me without thinking, I never even thought about them. Every part of me and every piece of equipment were non-existent; I just *was*. My skates were my feet, my gloves and stick were my hands and my pads were my skin. When I was in the Zone, I knew they would work for me. I never even thought that I carried around 30 pounds of equipment until it was all in one bag and I had to lug it to the car.

# My Experiment

I knew that somehow I had to get to that same level of subconscious competence in karate. Somehow I had to trust that my arms and feet would take care of me, that they would automatically do what I had spent years training them to do — block kicks and punches and deliver offensive power — without having to think about it at all.

I can honestly tell you that I initially had no idea how to get to this skill level. But an idea occurred to me — another experiment. Where I got the idea I'll never know but it was one of those ideas that seemed good at the time. So, in my next practice, I made a conscious decision to stop blocking any and all attacks, both kicks and punches. Now, this experiment was performed in the relative safety of a karate practice, although none of my opponents were let in on what I was doing — nor, I presume, would they have cared.

My experiment was not without risk. Although no contact to the head was allowed, we usually permitted "some" body contact during sparring. The higher the belt level, the more contact you got and were expected to take. So, as the first match commenced, I took one hard hit after another. I side-stepped to avoid attacks and remained resolutely block-less. I made every effort to "not think" about blocking, no matter what. In this case, it hurt a great deal to "not think".

# It Worked

After several fights, my fellow karate practitioners showed no signs of acknowledging my blocking incompetence, nor did they show sympathy. They had me in pain — my ribs hurt, by chest had welts caused by knuckles twisting my gi (tunic or uniform) — and I imagine they were enjoying it! But underlying my pain I felt a strange sensation. It grew stronger from match to sparring match, stronger and stronger, until — I'm not sure when or in what fight it happened — I exploded with a bewildering barrage of punches and kicks at one of my opponents. *Wow,* I remember saying to myself, *this is cool.* And I did it without thinking.

My explanation is this: In the midst of this painful process, my subconscious mind must have gotten frustrated and angry, and then rebelled, as if to say, "If you are not going to block, I will!" Whatever the explanation, it was the turning point in my career and I never had to think about blocking again — my subconscious mind did it for me from that point on. I had only to set the offensive outcome of winning and my arms and legs and body knew exactly what to do and when. It was the kind of TRUST I would bring to every future competition. It was subconscious competence!

# Exercises: TRUST BUILDING

In all clay target sports, you must TRUST in your abilities as well as in the tools you have learned in this book. There can be no thought or self-talk. Your shotgun must simply be an extension of your arms. You must learn to let your subconscious mind shoot the target. Dropping targets and correcting for them via correction routines will perfect it. The following are some exercises that will help you to learn to trust your skills and to build subconscious competence. Like me, experiment with these exercises to move your game to the level of TRUST required to win.

**1) Get yourself so exhausted you can hardly stand up.** It is a lot cheaper to do this by physical activity — a two-hour workout, plus a five-mile run, plus 100 pushups — than by shooting 1000 birds. Then, without resting, go out on the range, focus purely on getting your Zone, do your pre-shot routines and shoot. Your conscious mind will be so focused on overcoming your exhaustion — your labored breathing, heavy arms and shaky legs — that thinking will be impossible. (Only do this if you are fit and healthy and with a doctor's approval.)

**2) As you shoot, mentally visualize some other activity, like the swimmer's breaststroke.** Get in the Zone and then occupy your conscious mind with the breaststroke, and call for target after target. Stay with the breaststroke and see if you can get your subconscious mind smoking the targets for you. Oh, and enjoy the swim.

**3) Pick one basic target and shoot it over and over.** Anytime you get tired, bored or frustrated, stop for a moment and resolve the emotions with one of the tools you have learned. Proceed in this manner until shifting back to the Zone becomes automatic.

**4) Wear an iPod and listen to music.** With some attention to volume level so as not to damage your hearing, get in the Zone by concentrating on the emotion of the music. With your conscious mind nicely distracted, your subconscious mind will be free to do the shooting for you.

**5) Step into a station and visualize several targets breaking exactly where you want them to break.** Now, when you are completely wired to shoot and ready (with lots of adrenaline), call for the target but refuse to shoot. Call for another and refuse to shoot. Do this several times until you can feel — like I did in karate — your subconscious mind engage and initiate the process, as if to have your subconscious mind say, "If you aren't going to break the target, I will."

The objective of these exercises is to distract the conscious mind from the shooting task and to let your subconscious mind do what it is good at. You want to be running on automatic. It is a fantastic feeling where you shoot without thinking. The gun is a part of you and could just as easily be your arm. The reload is so fluid that it is automatic. The call for the bird — was that you who said it?

# Chapter Summary

By TRUSTING in your abilities first, you can develop your skills so that nothing, not even distracting comments from your peers, can affect you or your Zone. In the next chapter we'll take all that we have learned and create an unflappable attitude so that missing a target, or several, or completely falling apart becomes part of the learning experience — something to laugh about.

# 25 Now that's Attitude

*"When someone tells me there is only one way to do things, it always lights a fire under my butt. My instant reaction is, I'm gonna prove you wrong."*

### — Picabo Street, Star Skier

I work with many different sports and many great passionate athletes, but I get a few that require attitude adjustments. They simply lack that same kind of passion. This kind of athlete makes any number of excuses for not winning (and sometimes even for winning). They relate failure to coaches, parents, equipment and even the weather. A few rightfully place the blame squarely on their own shoulders but even this can be counterproductive. Blaming, making excuses and targeting oneself are only helpful from the perspective of your opponents (i.e., they don't have to do it to you if you're doing it to yourself).

## Passion Trumps Skill

Give me a passionate athlete with limited skills anytime over one who is disinterested yet has fabulous skills. I've been working with just such athlete over several years — a young hockey player — the one who is heading to pro-camp. He has passion, tenacity and a never-say-die attitude. Initially he had limited confidence, but slowly and surely he developed into a skillful, dynamic and confident athlete.

He also had many disappointments, such as the time he failed to make the state team. Afterwards, his dad told me that camp had gone well and he'd never seen his son play better. It had been a tremendous experience for him, and yet he suspected his son might be greatly disappointed. Hence, when he asked me to speak to him, I was expecting the worst.

In our next clinic, the young man spoke excitedly of the training camp, the mental training he had gotten, the high intensity scrimmages and the opportunity to raise his game to another level by playing with many other talented athletes. He had a fire in his eyes and I was pleased by his exuberance. I asked him what he wanted to do next. "I want to get better," he said. "I now know I need to be a smarter player." I smiled. Here he was giving me the pep talk. Now that's ATTITUDE!

# View of the World

Attitude — how you view the world — is critically important as it affects your resiliency. You immediately forget mistakes and move on, or you carry them for the rest of the competition, perhaps all your life. There are so many things that can negatively affect your game. Friends or parents may be watching. A blistering hot day may cause dehydration and fatigue. An adjustment to your gun mount is awkward and bothersome. An old sports injury acts up. And with all or some of the above, you could still show great ATTITUDE by sticking to your game.

On another day, everything goes well. There was something special in the coffee. Your squad mates are all in the Zone. Camaraderie is fantastic. Targets seem as big as garbage pail lids. You get lots of slaps on the back as you smoke targets without thinking. And you show "great" ATTITUDE by walking around tall and encouraging others.

We are initially oblivious to our ATTITUDE. We bounce back when we're young, just as we bounced back from repeated falling when we learned to walk. Then, after a certain age, we start to become self-conscious of how we perform. We search for reasons for awful performances, such as blaming others, blaming ourselves, creating excuses. If we are used to being great because of inferior opponents or because of our ability, when the game gets a little more competitive our self-worth may get tainted by failure. We get embarrassed, defensive and impatient with ourselves and others. Our self-worth gets tied to our score, and we can begin to show some serious ATTITUDE defects, such as throwing husks. No one wants us around.

# The Loop: Outcome, GPS, Tools

In order to prevent ATTITUDE from degenerating into anti-social behaviors, we need to take advantage of every experience — losses, mistakes and even wins. We need to know our OUTCOME, and that we will eventually get what we want, as perceived with DÉJÀ-VU. We need to understand that everything is GPS — and nothing is bad, negative, stupid or makes us an inferior human being. And we need to always act on GPS with TOOLS — FUSING, TALENT MODE, VISTA, and so on, and never quit.

Every experience gives you GPS and reveals information that, once processed, can propel you toward your OUTCOME. In the absence of blaming, beating yourself up, gloating etc., you have an incredible opportunity to learn. By stopping the negative from creeping in, you start to perceive the obvious and the subtle — and everything in between.

The young hockey player is an example of this. After every game he asks, "How can I get better and smarter?" With every injury he asks, "How can I get stronger and stay injury free?" And with very person who pulls him out of the Zone, he asks, "What can I do to prevent that or intimidate them instead?" The diagram illustrates how this kind of thinking keeps looping back in a way that moves us closer and closer to our outcome, when we are persistent.

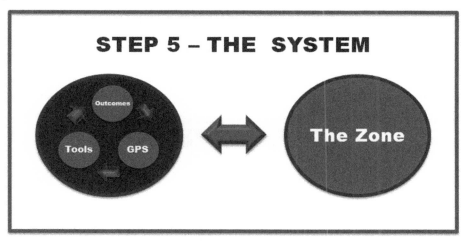

This is a simple process that, when displayed to those around us, comes across as great attitude. There is never frustration or doubt about the outcome. Getting cut in hockey or dropping targets in clay target sports is simply GPS. The athlete acts on the GPS by using technical or mental strategies and then tests out the changes. Each change gets him or her closer to the outcome and the loop begins again. That, in essence, is a great, never-say-die ATTITUDE.

## Exercise: ATTITUDE in Action

Since everyone can see ATTITUDE in other people's postures, let's use this measure in an attitude-building exercise for ourselves:

**1) Remember a less-than-stellar performance in your clay target shooting.** Step back and examine your image closely using the MIND COACH. Notice the tension or the hang-dog look or the redness in your face due to frustration. Then take another mental image, this time of an All-American, AAA or Master Class shotgunner, put him or her on the same field beside you and compare his or her image to your own. What do you notice? What are the differences? (Size or brightness, etc.)

**2) Once you have a clear idea of the differences, make some changes to the image of yourself.** That's right. Simply "redraw" your mental image. Make yourself look skillful by using TALENT MODE. Use FUSING to bring in some powerful past experiences. If the image appears too dark or distant or fuzzy, use VISTA to make it crystal clear and bright and focused. If you think it still looks a bit lame, press your A-Button.

**3) Once you are satisfied with the similarity of your image to the elite shooter, step onto the stage into the shoes of the new you and then go test it out on the range.**

**4) At various stages in your shooting year, reassess this image and continue to evolve into the shooter you wish to become.**

When you do this exercise you are acting on various forms of GPS, both the good and the bad. It is up to you to stay in the posture of the elite shooter through thick and thin. After every competition, you can re-evaluate how you did and loop back through the process. Like any strategy, it takes practice; it takes persistence; and it takes attitude. Rather, it *IS* ATTITUDE.

## Chapter Summary

Various attitudes such as blaming, using excuses, beating ourselves up or bragging (with a loss or a win) cloud our ability to challenge ourselves to become skillful shotgunners and keen competitors. We need to KNOW our Outcomes, ACT on the GPS and continually APPLY correct Tools. When we KNOW, ACT and APPLY the SportExcel System fluidly, we will have the kind of ATTITUDE that will ensure we start to win consistently. And, in the next chapter, I'll explain how dealing with the trauma of failure not only builds ATTITUDE, it is also the only way we can gain perspective and grow.

# 26 Attitude in Action

### Post-Traumatic Growth

*"You miss 100% of the shots you never take."*

— **Wayne Gretzky, Star Hockey Player**

B efore coming to see me, a few of my clients have been so discouraged that they asked themselves why they bothered to compete, why they put themselves on the line in front of their peers, why they accepted humiliation and then came back for more.

This human, competitive nature of needing to compete and needing to compare your ability to another's is very intriguing. It is helpful to have a great ATTITUDE from the outset in order to get through the trauma that can result from our need to compete and compare. Having great attitude shows you can process information subconsciously in a critical manner, with maturity and wisdom — the "glass half full" kind of competitor.

# Shotgunner vs Comic

Being a competitive shotgunner is very similar to being a stand-up comic. The disciplines have four things in common:

- When they miss, the result is immediately evident.
- They have hecklers (sometimes merely imagined but not always).
- They require good timing (skill).
- And, importantly, the only way to learn how to perform is to get up there and fail — the more times the better.

Although I have described how DÉJÀ-VU is a great aid in preparing for competitions, the only way to get realistic guidance for your mistakes is to learn "on the job." Initially, comics tell jokes poorly or misread the audience and get heckled. Initially, clay target shooters have poor skills or misread the targets and accept "friendly" barbs. Both put their honor, pride, self-esteem and man/womanhood on the line each time. And yet there is no other sensation quite like it, no other way to do it and we all love it when we're on and even when we're not.

"What is a grown man like me doing standing up here in front of my peers making a fool of myself?" is the question one trap shooter asked after his first few disastrous experiences. Coupled with his negative self-talk were a churning stomach, gurgling bowels, and a body soaked with sweat externally and adrenaline internally. He was quite delighted to hear that there is a term for his trial by fire — Post Traumatic Growth, the flip side to the Post-Traumatic Stress Disorder we hear so much about in the news, especially in regards to returning service men and women. In sports, Post Traumatic Growth (PTG) justifies our putting ourselves in "harm's way" with the expectation (vision) that we will eventually get that perfect score.

# Post Traumatic Growth

"Post-traumatic growth is a process people go through in the aftermath of experiencing trauma," said Dr. Robert Tedeschi, Professor of Psychology at the University of North Carolina at Charlotte when he addressed the Command and General Staff, college students and staff at Fort Leavenworth, Kansas. "It's also an outcome of trauma. It's a series of changes people experience themselves that they label as valuable, or beneficial, maybe not right away, but in the long run. Traumatic experience can be transformative in some people, putting them on a whole new life path."

What this suggests is that people have the ability to learn from their experiences, no matter how traumatic. The words of Friedrich Neitzsche, "What doesn't kill you makes you stronger," come to mind. The difficulty with concepts like PTG is that they are bandied around as "throw-away" speech topics by motivational speakers and few of these speakers actually know how to teach the rest of us the specifics of how to turn trauma into opportunities for growth.

Losing a round can be traumatic; taking the flak from your friends on your squad can be traumatic; the embarrassment of telling your spouse how poorly you did can be traumatic; wasting away at a plateau in a lower class while your colleagues have moved on can be traumatic. Perhaps these traumas are not on the scale of the human trauma that Dr. Tedeschi is talking about but it is the same process and the tools you have learned in this book will help you to grow beyond it.

## A New Way of Thinking

You have learned tools that will help you to shrink any problem.   You have learned a new way of thinking, one that allows you to evaluate your performance, no matter how bad the pain is.   You have learned to set your own path to what you want with DÉJÀ-VU DVD.   You have learned to see the world from the viewpoint of elite athletes through Talent Mode.   You have learned to step back and be the spectator of how others affect you via Mind Coach.   And, with all the other tools you have learned — FUSING, Power Walk, Power Shift, VISTA and the A-Button, you know how to make adjustments and move on.   No longer do you have to despair over the prospect of shooting poorly.

Lose or win, you can take all the tools the SportExcel System has to offer and incorporate these tools into your game at the subconscious level so that you grow in your ability to perform before, during and after your competition. The more you do to put yourself on the line in everything you do, the more you gain — Post Traumatic Gain.

## Chapter Summary

So, whether you are getting people to laugh as a stand-up comic, or getting them to stop laughing as a clay target shooter, you are pushing yourself to overcome trauma and exercising your potential for growth.  To quote Dr. Tedeschi again, "It's not the trauma that changes people, it's the struggle." The SportExcel System will help you with your own personal and performance struggles in shotgunning, in life and in your relationships.  In the last chapter, I'll put the responsibility to grow squarely in your court because the tools I've been teaching you don't do the work, you do. You now have the means to transform your game.

When fixing your blocks becomes easy, a winning attitude becomes automatic. Practice the tools.

Reference: Dr. Robert Tedeschi, Professor of Psychology at the University of North Carolina, Charlotte to the *Command and General Staff, college students and staff about "Posttraumatic Growth and Combat: Seeing possibilities for growth and ways of promoting it" in the Lewis and Clark Center's Eisenhower Auditorium, Fort Leavenworth, Kansas.*

http://www.army.mil/-news/2010/04/09/37139-expert-discusses-benefits-of-post-traumatic-growth/

# Step 6

## The Beginning:

### *A System that works when you do*

*"You are never really playing an opponent. You are playing yourself, your own highest standards, and, when you reach your limits that is real joy."*

— **Arthur Ash, Star Tennis Player**

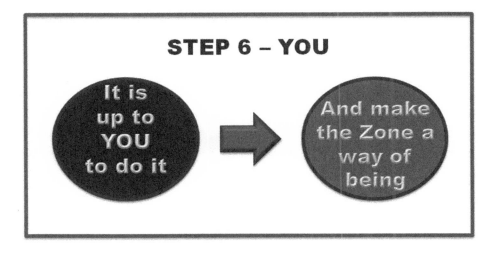

# 27 All About You (Applying the System)

## *Enjoy the Zone and Go Play — in Practice and in Competition*

*"I always practice as I intend to play."*

**— Jack Nicklaus, Star Golfer**

This, the final chapter, is when most books draw conclusions and draw to an end. But for you it is the beginning, the start of new perceptions, strategies, outlooks and outcomes. This is where we establish a commitment to excellence, where to paraphrase Vince Lombardi, we strive for perfection and settle for excellence.

You now have a beginning, a system that works like no other, to help you to win by getting you in the Zone and keeping you there. The tools of the system are very powerful, and — based on my findings and results with hundreds of athletes and many thousands of hours of training — easy to learn and apply. My athletes win; my coaches win. The insights and practical applications of the SportExcel System have resulted in many positive changes in teams and athletes — personal bests, great relationships, rewarding experiences, business leadership skills, educational enhancement, balanced lives and other bonuses of competing and coaching to win.

## Many Have Come Before You

Mike Westjohn is an example of this. In all his years of shooting, he studied the mental game. He took Tai Chi and read extensively to gain the edge. The SportExcel System helped him put it all together.

John (not his real name) is a youth example. He was already shooting against the best and simply needed consistency, especially against those his own age. He got more than he expected, as he learned leadership and was able to apply it to his high school sports as well, in a standout year.

Greg Elliot is a parent example of being the emotional ballast for his son. He and his wife learned to support their son in spectacular ways, mostly by simply staying in the Zone.

Les Greevy, USA Shooting Coach of the Year 2004, is a coaching example. He told me that he learned how important it was for him to stay in the Zone at a competition to enable his shooters to perform well. And do they ever!

Paul Giambrone III, Gil and Vicki Ash, Steve and Janet Brown and Don Kwasnycia are all examples of coaches who have all experienced new ways of perceiving the Zone and have used it to the benefit of the sport and their athletes.

Most of all, all these athletes and coaches who have learned the system have been a joy to work with and, in turn, have taught me so, so much.

# The New Way — a Repeatable System

Now, having read the book, you possess what each of these shotgunners and coaches possess, a new way of looking at the clay target sports within a repeatable system in six steps. Like them, you have Step 1 of the SportExcel System, the Zone, and the means to get into it via Zone FEEL and NO-Zone FEEL, both absolutely critical signals. They give you every opportunity to live in the Zone, all the time, no excuses.

You now know the importance of Step 2 of the SportExcel System, of having your OUTCOME bright and bold and adrenalized — DÉJÀ VU. Outcomes made real.

You now know the importance of Step 3 of the SportExcel System, of utilizing the good, the bad and the ugly as GPS or guidance. What doesn't kill you makes you stronger.

You now know the importance of Step 4 of the SportExcel System, and the tools that can flip you back into the Zone in the blink of the eye. You have FUSING to help you forget, TALENT MODE to help you to learn, VISTA to help make targets bigger, MIND COACH to help to lead or deal with others, POWER WALK to utilize you posture and POWER SHIFT to help maintain your Zone in action. And you have the A-Button to control your adrenaline. It is quite the tool kit. Use it.

You now know the importance of putting it all together at the subconscious level with Step 5 of the SportExcel System, where you loop through the system and get stronger and more skillful. Ultimately, through setting proper outcomes, testing them out in practice and competition and breaking through blocks and frustration time and again, you'll understand that losing your Zone FEEL is simply GPS — the symptom — and now have the means — the tools — to move on.

# All Sports, All Disciplines

The SportExcel System works with all sports: clay target shooting, soccer, golf, baseball, football, etc. It also works with business, the arts, healthcare, education and any other discipline you can think of. It is purely educational, not an attempt to fix you with psychology. It is strategy-based, just as mathematics is number and equation-based. You will not be "fixed" by this high performance approach, but you will now have a solid foundation of strategies with which to train yourself and to be competitive at any level, any age.

# It Doesn't Work, You Do

So, take your new tools and apply them — on every part of your game. Be skeptical if you must, but give the system a chance. This is Step 6 of the SportExcel System. The system doesn't work, you do. The tools don't work, you do. And, in order for you to work, you need to practice.

As I mentioned earlier, create a calendar for your training schedule and put a different tool at the top of each day — DÉJÀ VU on Monday, FUSING on Tuesday, TALENT MODE on Wednesday, etc. On that day, practice that tool over and over until it becomes easy to use. On the next day, practice the next tool, and so on. Every time you apply a tool, it will become easier to use and ultimately will become so ingrained in your subconscious that it will be applied instantly in a crisis, just as quickly as the answer of 2 + 2 comes to mind.

Here are a few parting shots:

- As you are now fully on the road to excellence, you may want to go on this journey with someone: A clay target coach. No matter how good your mental game is, or how mature you are, or how successful you are in other sports or business, everyone needs a coach. The cost will be worth it.

- Stay healthy on this journey — eat healthy, drink in moderation, throw away the smokes, etc. You know the routine. If for no other reason, do it to maintain your visual acuity as you grow older. Besides, it just feels good being healthy.

- The Zone is a skill, and just like any other skill, it needs to be practiced.

- Enjoy the Zone and go have some fun with practice and play — and win. Winning is not the only reason you will want to continue with your sport, as more often than not enjoyment is a pretty high requirement. But winning was an essential ingredient for me and I suspect for you as well. Go for it.

- Call me if you want more guidance (one-on-one training, training tune-ups, parent/young athlete training or in-person clinics) as I'm very good at GPS when you have overlooked something.

- And last, if anyone tells you to set realistic goals because only 1% of clay target shooters will ever be World or Grand Champions, I say, YOU strive to be the 1%.

I wish you great shooting, great enjoyment, and great growth, whatever your sport and whatever your projected level of attainment. If you would like more information about the SportExcel System or resources to back up your training library including DVDs, audio CDs and training programs, please contact me toll-free in North America at 1.800.967.5747, international at 705.720.2291 or email: bpalmer@sportexcel.ca and/or visit my website: www.sportexcel.ca.

# Biography

## Bob Palmer, B.Ed., B.E.S.

**CEO, High Performance Strategist and Trainer, SportExcel Inc.**

Bob Palmer founded SportExcel Inc. in 1994, driving 21st century high-performance innovation that is transforming how athletes, coaches and sports organizations achieve their dreams. A respected and inspiring industry leader and expert, Palmer has been instrumental in pioneering a non-psychology approach that is revolutionizing the sports industry.

The SportExcel system has been embraced by a wide range of sports including the clay target sports, surfing, snowboarding, skateboarding, triathlon and golf as well as the team sports of football, hockey, baseball and soccer. It has ignited the passion, joy and skillfulness of athletes and coaches. Athletes in a number sports, including the shooting sports, have achieved podium success in the Olympics, PanAm, Commonwealth and X Games as a result.

A 4th degree black belt, Palmer is a member of the Shintani Wado Kai Karate Association where he currently holds the position of High Performance Trainer for the Shintani Wado Kai Karate National Team. He is also a member of the Coaches Association of Ontario and has previously served as the Chairman of the Barrie Sports Hall of Fame, on the board of Big Brothers and as a volunteer with the YMCA.

A professional educator, Palmer holds a degree in Education from Brock University, a degree in Environmental Studies from the University of Waterloo and a Master Practitioner level in neuro-linguistic training. He writes on high performance and leadership for Trap & Field Magazine, Skeet Shooting Review and several on-line magazines and newsletters.

SportExcel Inc. is reinventing and rejuvenating the world of sport high performance. For more information, visit www.sportexcel.ca or call 877.967.5747.